DEVIL AT THE WHEEL

Other current books by Gordon McLean:

How To Raise Your Parents and Other Helpful Advice for Teen-agers

God, Help Me, I'm a Parent

Where the Love Is

Let God Manage Your Money

Hell-Bent Kid

Fear Thy Neighbor

Man, I Need Help

DEVIL AT THE WHEEL

Gordon McLean
with Ken Pestana

DIMENSION BOOKS
BETHANY FELLOWSHIP, INC.
Minneapolis, Minnesota

Devil at the Wheel
by Gordon McLean
with Ken Pestana

Library of Congress Catalog Card Number 74-28547

ISBN 0-87123-101-8

Copyright © 1975
Bethany Fellowship, Inc.
All Rights Reserved

All pictures in this book are used by permission of
Family Films, Inc., producers of the motion picture,
Devil at the Wheel.

DIMENSION BOOKS
Published by Bethany Fellowship, Inc.
6820 Auto Club Road, Minneapolis, Minnesota 55438

Printed in the United States of America

To
Angelo Pestarino and
Russell Roessler,
who came to represent a client
and stayed to be friends

Foreword

On these pages you will meet a young man who had to reach bottom before he would look up. I can relate to that situation. For Ken Pestana it took a murder charge to climax a short, spectacular series of crimes. For me it took a career that was close to ruin, a family that split up, and the devastating effects of pills and booze.

The prayers of some concerned friends were with me and those prayers were answered. In 1970 I made a complete rededication of my life to Jesus Christ, having been initially introduced to the Lord at the age of twelve.

I have more than a career; I also have a ministry. Among various opportunities for service, I have given many special programs in prisons, and I can understand where the inmates are coming from. I know the hopelessness and despair they face, but I also know the power of God that can change even the hardest among them.

I am concerned about young people. June and I are deeply committed to Christian youth work, and I have come to especially appreciate the ministry of Youth for Christ and men in that ministry like Ken Overstreet in San Diego and Gordon McLean in San Jose. I am glad they are ministering to all kinds of young people, including the young man in this book.

Society is often at a loss to know what to do with people like Ken Pestana. That's one reason his story is so interesting. But this is much more than a crime thriller; it is the true story of the power of God to reshape a young rebel, the story of hope in the middle of tragedy.

When you finish this book I trust you will see beyond a teen-ager charged with murder to the reality of the power of God to transform a life that is responsive to Him.

What the Lord seeks is an open door—then a new life begins. A young man in big trouble found it. So can anyone else. That is the message on these pages.

Johnny Cash

Preface

"What is Gordon McLean doing these days?" a friend of mine asked Ken Pestana.

"He's working with a murderer, an armed robber, a conspirator, and, oh yes, an extortionist," Ken replied.

This seemed very serious indeed to my friend even though he knew I was in Christian ministry, often working with young people in trouble with the law. "You mean he's counseling four young people charged with crimes like those?"

"No," calmly explained Ken, "just one guy—me."

It was true, and working with that young man was one of the most unusual, emotionally trying, educational and rewarding experiences of my life. But frankly, at first I had no plans to publish anything about what began as an ordinary, though tragic, crime and arrest.

The book finally resulted from several things, among them a conference I had with a high-level law enforcement official in his private office. He called me in, shut the door, and spoke directly.

"Look, you've tried to help many young people who have broken the law. We haven't always agreed on that subject, but you and I had our jobs to do and we did them. We're friends and that's why I'm talking to you. I understand that you now have Ken Pestana in your program. Let me warn you—you're making a big mistake. That fellow is nothing but a loser; he's a slick con artist.

"Worse, he's up against the most serious charges. I think it's a mistake for him to be out on bail before trial. Who knows what he'll do next. And frankly, we believe he's been in on other jobs that he's never been charged with. Don't let that guy tell you he's some kind of an angel; he's not. I'm telling you this as a friend. I know it's your business, but I just don't want to see you get hurt."

Indeed, the man was motivated by a desire to be helpful, and I thanked him for that. But I could not accept his advice and was frustrated at being unable to answer his statements. I thought of doing it later in a written report.

At that time I could not tell him Ken's problems were no secret to me. For example, I didn't have to read the records to learn of Ken's conduct at the county boys' ranch. I was there day-by-day seeing the problems as they arose. And when Ken was getting into trouble, I made it very clear that I approved of neither his conduct nor his attitude.

When Ken was released from the ranch, I kept in limited contact with him, which only confirmed my firm belief that he was heading for more serious trouble. But even then there was a tacit understanding between us: he never tried to mislead me into thinking he was anything but a young ruffian, and I made clear my desire to rechannel in positive ways his good mind and talents. But I never confused goals with reality; I knew exactly where Ken stood.

It took a tragic murder charge to break our

deadlock and move Ken in the direction God intended the youth to go. This is the story of that experience. And while it was happening, Ken opened his heart to me, his family, his past, and his friends for as close a scrutiny as one person can ever have of another. Never did he evade a question or equivocate with an answer. Much as it may amaze some of the authorities, I believe my almost daily talks with Ken were totally frank and honest.

Most of our conversations could have been held within the strict confines of ministerial confidence, and this book would never have been written. But Ken did not ask that our communication be treated as privileged information, and when we decided to prepare the material on these pages, he insisted that everything be included—the bad with the good. It is.

I watched this young man change under the most unbelievable pressures. Though he had the finest legal counsel, the major court decisions were his alone, choices that could affect years of his life. He chose to change his choice of friends, his habits, his attitude, his language, his wardrobe—in fact, his whole life-style. While he was going through this transformation, he had to face people who either didn't believe he was changing or they were convinced it was only a front and a sham.

No man alone can work a total change of his life. The desire may be there, but it takes divine intervention to effectively and totally restructure a shattered life. Many people, if they are inclined to accept the validity of Christian conversion at all, think that sort of intervention stopped in Bible times with Paul on the road to Damascus. But God is still changing people, and today millions of men and women can testify to the reality of an encounter with Jesus Christ. I'm in that number, and now so is Ken Pestana.

Ken still makes mistakes and has much to learn; he is the first to admit that. There is no doubt that he has a long ways to go in the Christian life, but it is amazing that he ever started in at all.

Meeting and knowing Ken as you will on these pages is one thing; feeling sorry for him is another. Neither he nor I want sympathy. Most of the problems in which he finds himself are of his own making, and he must face the consequences for his conduct. That he is doing.

Any sympathy here must go to the family and loved ones of another young man, the store clerk who so tragically and unnecessarily was killed during what is normally the happiest season of the year—Christmas time. Our prayers for God's love and sustaining strength are with those who lost one who was very dear to them.

As I mentioned, neither Ken nor I planned to write a book. Only when so many unusual events kept happening to lift Ken's story from the level of a crime and courtroom thrill story to a vivid witness for our Lord did we decide to write it. And I saw "we" advisedly, for Ken spent many hours helping prepare these pages.

Ken's attorneys, his family, his friends on both sides of the law, as well as Jim Thibodeux from our Youth for Christ/Campus Life staff and Sergeant David Pascual of the Santa Clara County Sheriff's office were most helpful.

Richard Bothman, chief juvenile probation officer, and his staff at the county James Boys Ranch gave us valuable help.

In completing the book, my thanks go to Clyde Vandeburg, Art Linkletter, and Leslie Renta for assisting in publicaton and promotion of this book as well as another of my books, and to another good friend, Johnny Cash, for his kind introduction. Grace Francone and my secretary, Madelynn Moran, spent long hours typing and preparing the manuscript. Scripture quotations are from *The Way*, an edition of the Living Bible prepared by the editors of *Campus Life Magazine* and published by Tyndale House.

Most of the single first names are fictionalized. The full names are real and all of the incidents described are true to the best of my knowledge, based on careful research of police and court records as well as numerous interviews with those involved.

While I am most grateful for the assistance mentioned in preparing this book, I alone am responsible for the information and views written on these pages, and those who helped should not be considered as endorsing the views expressed here.

Gordon R. McLean
San Jose, California

CONTENTS

1. Hurry Up, Mister, or I'll Kill You! 17
2. I'm Going to Be Here a Long Time 29
3. Get Ready for the Big Payback 39
4. I'm the Young Gangster in Big Trouble 51
5. God, You and Me Are So Far Apart 65
6. You're Not the Guy I Used to Know 77
7. Wonderful to Know You're Loved 89
8. Somebody Up There Likes You 108
9. Everybody Has a Master 126
   Epilogue 139

Gordon McLean and Ken Vestalia talking during a break in the filming of the movie.

CHAPTER 1

"Hurry Up, Mister, or I'll Kill You!"

"Hey Kenny, that guy you were talking to the other day wants to buy a jar of reds from you. I gave him your number, and he's going to call you in a few minutes."

"Yeah, okay, I'll talk to him. I think we can do a little business."

As Ken hung up the phone, his buddy Al called from the other room, "Who's that on the phone?"

"Just Marilyn telling me about this dude who wants some reds. The guy is going to call here."

"Good deal," commented Al, coming into the kitchen. "Let's burn the cat. You ain't got no reds, but we can still get his money. If he wants a jar of reds, he's gotta have $120 to pay for them."

"You got a point. I ain't too hip on being without money," Kenny replied.

"Tell him to meet us at Sambo's at 6:30 tonight," Al ordered. "We'll be ready."

Ken was more than a little uneasy over the idea. Since the fellow was a starter, Ken really didn't want to burn the guy. Then, too, he wasn't sure just how much his young partner might do. Al was tense and erratic. Worst of all, he constantly talked of using weapons—a veritable arsenal of firearms which he had collected in a string of burglaries.

Ken was staying at his uncle's house where the fellow wanting the reds soon called, having obtained Ken's number from Marilyn.

The meeting was set and Ken concluded, "Be on time at 6:30. If I'm not there, don't wait. Bogey on."

Ken hung up and called to Al, "We're in business. The guy will meet us at 7."

"Tell you what, Ken," Al suggested, "why don't you pick up Slim and have him join us? He might enjoy this."

Ken agreed, jumped into his truck and drove off to pick up the third youth. When the pair returned they walked into the house to face Al with a sawed-off shotgun aimed at them, both barrels ready to fire. Al started laughing. This was his idea of a joke.

The three fellows hopped into Kenny's pickup and left. It was December 27 in the area of San Jose, California. The stage was now set for a tragedy which was to go far beyond that of threatening a would-be drug buyer to turn over a few bucks.

Slim, aged seventeen, was the product of a divided home. His mother had worked hard to make up for the lacks of an indifferent and often cruel father who finally left the family. But the damage to the boys was difficult to repair.

Al, sixteen, was no stranger to the loneliness and hate which had been building inside him for a long time and now all but possessed him. One of eight children, his parents, due partly to illness, had been unable to raise him or the older boys. Al was in a boys' ranch twice and several foster homes, one of them a concerned Christian family who tried very hard to help him. But Al's problems were deep rooted and severe; he was a very withdrawn young man. The only time Al saw his father in many years was in court, and on that occasion Al didn't even recognize him.

Al stayed at the boys' school for a long sixteen months while the officials tried to find a placement for him. When he was placed, it didn't work out well or for long. He quit school, roamed the streets, stayed a few days here and there with various friends, and stole to make his way. He was good at it too.

Money and some valuables could always take care of him for a while. But he soon began collecting guns and other weapons from the houses he burglarized until he had built up a pretty big arsenal of weapons and ammunition. His most prized weapon was a $4,000 shotgun he had sawed off and now carried in the back of Ken's pickup. He was drinking too, so his memory of the events of this tragic night was later to be vague at times.

Ken Pestana, eighteen and no longer a juvenile, was the oldest. Dark featured, strong, wiry, proud of his long black hair, deliberately casual in his dress, Ken divided his time between working on the engine or body of his pickup truck and making the local Saratoga scene with a steady succession of girls. School or work rarely made his priority list.

That was the trio: A young guy looking for

excitement, another armed with a powerful weapon and filled with hatred, and a daredevil driver who loved to play the gangster role. They made for a wild combination. It was soon to prove a deadly one.

Before they split from the house, Al explained the plan. "We meet the guy at the restaurant. I'll stay in the back of the truck under the tarp so the guy doesn't see me. Ken, you tell him to pick any quiet place he wants to make the deal on the reds and we'll drive to wherever he says. Then you park the truck and walk away from it with Slim and the guy. I'll sneak out of the back, come around on you guys, pretend to hold all three of you up and we'll get his money."

"Not bad," said Slim. "But be sure to make it look good."

"Don't worry," replied Al, cradling the sawed-off shotgun. "I'll rough you guys up a little bit when I'm taking your wallets; then I'll cut out. You can give the guy a lift to a nearby street and talk about what a tough break it was for all of you to get ripped off. He won't even ask for the reds, which Kenny don't have anyway."

Slim didn't say much, but Ken was more than a little uneasy. "But suppose the guy fights you or something?"

"If the guy gives me any back talk, I'll take care of him," Al calmly replied. Ken believed his partner would do exactly that. Ken wasn't so sure he really wanted to go through with the plan, but he had the uneasy feeling that raising an objection might make him the target for his buddy, so he kept quiet.

Ken never drank liquor, but he did fortify himself with some reds before the start of the evening's events. Al drank tequila.

"I had been dealing reds and it was no sweat to get the guy a jar. But I didn't feel like it that night. I could have used part of the $120, but something was wrong with this setup; it was just bad. I didn't want to see anyone get burned," Ken later explained.

The trio arrived at the restaurant at 7 p.m., but the guy they were to meet was nowhere around. Ken knew he wouldn't be, for he had deliberately set the contact time so they would not meet. Neither Slim nor Al knew what was happening.

"That guy isn't here," said Slim impatiently. "We'd better go back to the truck and tell Al."

"What's the big rush?" replied Ken. "Let's get a cup of coffee first. He may show up yet."

When the pair finally did return to the pickup and told their partner no one had met them, Al was furious.

"I've got to get some coin! I've got to be splitting from Kenny's uncle's pad in a few days before those people get back, and I just ain't gonna bogey up in the streets. I want some money to put me up for a while. I don't want to be walking the streets. I want a taxi to take me. Let's go find a store!"

"I know where there's a good one," Slim volunteered. "No one is there too much at night. Grab the wheel, Kenny, and I'll show you how to find it."

Slim knew what he was talking about. The

store he selected was off the main street in a quiet area surrounded by houses and a nearby school. Even at 7 in the evening there was very little in the way of business and customers.

Ken circled the area, drove slowly past the store, and then parked about a block away. Al jumped out of the back of the truck and said, "This shouldn't take more than a few minutes."

Ken didn't actually see the shotgun Al had under his old army jacket, but he knew his partner had the weapon.

In the store a few customers had just entered. Al waited for them to leave.

Slim and Ken, waiting impatiently in the truck, lit up a joint.

After what was only a few minutes but seemed much longer to the waiting pair, Al came running back to the pickup, jumped in and said, "Start the truck. We've got to split!"

The 7/Eleven Store in Cupertino involved in the murder-robbery case.

Ken, too stoned to respond to anything quickly, slowly drove off.

Al was talking fast. "It was bad. You'll never believe it. That scene is a real mess. Blood all over the wall and everything. I blew that store clerk away. One thing about this gun, when it fires, it really fires."

Ken was sobering up fast. He found it hard to believe what he was hearing. Slim, too, was stunned. Al showed his two buddies a bag filled with money.

"Here, check this out," Al continued. "I got ducats now, man."

"Hey, wait a minute," Ken responded, "you robbed that store. Right?"

Ken knew the store was going to be robbed, but he didn't really believe the clerk had been shot until Al emptied out the shells on the seat and reloaded the weapon. The smell of gun powder confirmed his worst suspicion.

"Wow, man! Let's get out of here!" said Ken, shoving the gas pedal to the floor.

Slim asked to go home but Al talked about another job. Ken and Slim weren't interested.

"Look, guys," the young man explained, "this was unbelievable. I walked in there and told the guy to do exactly what I told him. You ought to have seen the guy. He was begging me not to hurt him. I told him to get a bag and give me all bills, no coins. Then I said, 'Hurry up, mister, or I'll kill you!' The guy just started talking to me. He was real scared. He told me he had just worked there a few nights getting some money to pay for his college. The guy was all big, like an athlete. I'm just little beside him, but my shotgun did all the talking. He said, 'I didn't do nothing to you. You got my money. What else do you want?' He handed the bag of money to me and stepped back from the counter. I didn't know what he was going to do. I fired both barrels."

Slim and Ken dared not interrupt. They just listened in stunned silence. Al was pretty drunk but his two partners feared Al was telling the truth. Soon Ken pulled up in front of Slim's house and let off his two passengers.

Ken drove home, fixed himself something to eat, though he wasn't really hungry, and turned on the television news. The reporter soon told of the tragic death of a twenty-year-old college baseball player at a Seven-Eleven store in Cupertino. The amount taken was $104.16. According to the report, the police had some leads to go on. A university computer operator told the sheriff's officers that as he had passed by the store he had seen a flash and heard a bang. He had seen a youth walk out of the store, slip and fall, pick himself up and start running. The youth had a weapon about two feet long in his hand. He was also carrying a bag. He had long, blond hair and appeared to be about sixteen to eighteen years of age.

Unknown to Ken as he watched the news, the police had another valuable lead. A woman resident of the house in front of which Kenny had parked his pickup had, for no apparent reason, wondered about the strange vehicle and its two occupants. Acting on impulse, she had copied down the license number and a description of the truck and called it in to the authorities. The help of those two citizens was to prove vital in breaking the case.

But that night Ken and his buddies felt they had gotten clean away. And as for the police looking for a blond youth, age sixteen to eighteen, well, any number of guys would fit that description.

Marilyn was there when Kenny drove back to his uncle's house. He didn't talk much, just ate and watched the television news.

Later Al came over to the house in a taxi, and he was eager to go out again.

"Are you crazy, man?" Ken shouted. "You're on television. Every cop for miles is looking for you!"

Al was excited at being a news celebrity and quickly turned to the various channels to watch the late night news reports of his crime.

Another friend, Louis, showed up. "What have you guys been up to tonight?" he asked innocently.

"Nothing but murder," Al replied.

Marilyn joined Louis, and the stunned pair got a firsthand report of the evening's events from Al. Louis volunteered to get rid of the weapon by dumping it in a nearby lake. He left in Kenny's truck. The shotgun never got to the lake but was used later that same evening in another robbery. Only Louis or his pals can explain that incident.

When Ken learned the weapon hadn't been disposed of, he insisted on retrieving it and planned to bury it in the backyard of his uncle's home. He decided to wait until morning, and for the night hid the weapon in the chimney of the fireplace.

Shortly thereafter Kenny heard some noise and looked out the front window to see sheriffs' cars everywhere. "Oh, wow, this is a bust," he called out to Al. Al wanted to get out some of his guns but Ken protested, "Hey, man, take your pieces and split! They haven't got anything on me. You just split."

Al headed out the back door, forgot the swimming pool was there and fell in. He quickly pulled himself out and made it over the back fence as the police came to the front door.

Inside, Ken told Marilyn to get rid of the reds and the bag of money on the table. She hid the money behind the couch and put the reds in her purse.

The detective leading the officers came in and asked Kenny where he had been that evening in his truck.

"Just out bogeying around," Kenny replied. "Hey look, man, I know I got some traffic tickets I ain't paid, but I'll take care of them."

"We're not here about traffic tickets, Ken."

"Then what are you here for?"

"This is for murder."

"No man, you got the wrong cat. I don't know nothing about no murder. I'm tired now. I've got to get to bed."

"You're tired all right. We're taking you for a drive."

"Where?"

"Well suppose for openers you take us by the store where you stopped and parked around 7."

"Oh, yeah, I was out by a store. I had some

trouble with my tape deck so I stopped for a few minutes and fixed it."

Ken got into the detectives' car and drove to the area of the store and showed them where he had parked.

"Did you see anything suspicious when you were here?" an officer asked.

"Yeah, there were some hippy types hanging around."

"Okay, Ken, now we'll go downtown and get a statement."

"Hey, look man, I'm sick. Why don't you just take me home and let me go to bed."

But the sheriff's office is where they went. Ken was advised of his rights to remain silent and have counsel present for any questioning and then was told, "Let me lay this out for you. We know you didn't do the shooting. You don't match the description of the fellow we're looking for. But we do want to know what you know about it."

Kenny tried passing off a few fake stories, even claiming at one point he had done the shooting himself. But the detectives were not about to be deterred by such amateur attempts at lying. They got around to talking about Al. They believed he was their man.

"If you figure it's him, why ask me?" Ken responded. "He's sixteen, still a juvenile; you can't do much to him."

Al was only sixteen, but Ken's thoughts on juveniles were wrong. Al was soon to be caught, transferred from juvenile to adult court and face trial. Only Slim got the break and was tried as a juvenile.

Kenny was booked into the county jail. The charges were conspiracy, armed robbery, and murder. Three days later the death penalty was once again to become the law in California for such an offense. Al was too young to face the gas chamber, but Kenny missed that possibility by only a few days.

A tired, depressed young man was locked in the maximum security cells of murder row. He lay on his bunk tired but unable to sleep. "This is pretty heavy, man. I'm in for murder," Ken told himself.

Later Ken said to me, "Then I laughed. I guess to keep up my courage. But inside I cried. I was always the bad guy, the rough bad dude, but if I told the other guys in the jail how terrible I felt being in on a deal where a guy was killed, I'd ruin my image.

"So I kept up the front. But inside I wasn't laughing. I kept thinking about that guy getting blown away. I still wake up at night thinking about him. And all so that some young punks could get a lousy $104.16. And then I thought of the mess I was in."

The murder charge was Kenny's most serious bust. But it was not his first one.

Two years earlier he had spent some time at the county boys' ranch. That, too, had been a traumatic experience for the would-be young gangster. And it almost forecast the tragic events of this December night.

CHAPTER 2

"I'm Going to Be Here a Long Time"

"What kind of a place is this?" Ken asked the probation officer driving him across the bridge in to James Ranch in Morgan Hill, California. He didn't pay much attention to the answer.

At first glance the place didn't look too bad. The sight of a farm and animals seemed a strange setting to rehabilitate a sixteen-year-old tough guy from the urban streets. But there were no walls, gun towers, or even a fence. It was obvious that leaving the place would not present much of a challenge.

He was soon admitted, issued some ranch clothes, and told his hair would be cut. That was a point of real conflict. It took the effort of several counselors to get his long locks sheared.

Ken was angry and let the staff know it. "No one cuts my hair. I'm declaring war on you people. It's all of you against me from this point on. I'm going to be just as rough and rowdy as I can."

And Ken set out to prove that this was no idle boast.

"I really wanted to get out of that place. Some of my partners were up at the Youth Authority, and I figured if I could be sent there

I would have a lot less hassles.

"Besides there was my reputation to think about. If I got out and told my buddies I had been to the James Ranch, they would only laugh at me and say, 'That ain't nothin'.' Y.A. was different. That was a heavier trip and the guys would look up to me.

"But I decided not to escape right away. I'd stay at least long enough to figure out the ranch. I checked to see if there were any drugs around the campus. There weren't at that time. That was a letdown.

"I've read a lot about reform schools for kids around the country, and most of them are pretty bad—old buildings, poor staff, bad food, nothing to help the guys get straightened out. This place ain't nothing like that.

"They got a school program, sports, some work, home leaves, and some counselors who aren't just guards, but are there because they want to help guys with problems.

"I had the problems, but I didn't want the help."

It didn't take Ken and the ranch long to clash seriously. One of the senior wards, a boy in A-section, told Ken he was going to the office because he wasn't showing proper attitude and respect.

Ken, new and in C-section, promptly responded, "Listen, I've got just as much respect for you punk A boys as I have for the counselors here, and that ain't much."

A counselor overheard the remark and said, "Pestana, get in here. We've got to have a talk."

"Yeah, I think we do too," Ken replied,

sprawling out across a chair in the ranch dormitory office.

"Pestana, I know you don't like it here," the counselor said. "But you were sent here. It isn't my trip, it's yours. We can make it pleasant for you or we can make it very hard on you."

"Well, you go right ahead. I'm going to make it hard on you just like you're going to make it hard on me," Ken replied.

"I hear you've been going around asking the boys about where to get drugs here at the center," the counselor continued. "That kind of thing will get you into trouble and get you demoted. You'll get out of here when we think we've done all we can do to help you."

"Mister, I have the feeling I'm going to be here a long time."

"You know, Pestana, I kind of figured that when you walked in the door."

"What's your name?" Ken inquired.

"Bob Hedges, that's Mr. Hedges to you."

"Okay, I just wanted to know. You're number one on my enemy list."

The attitude and actions matched the talk—indifference at school, conflicts with the other boys, disruptions on work details.

Then came a confrontation with a supervisor who ordered Ken to clean up a mess he'd made in the dorm. "Clean it up yourself. I'm going to bed," Ken replied.

"Keep it up and you'll go to bed right back there in the isolation room," warned the supervisor.

"That's not bad," Ken fired back; "just think, a private room all to myself."

A few days later on an outside work detail Ken and Mr. Hedges again clashed. This time Ken, shovel in hand, came upon the counselor, ready to attack the man. One of the boys shouted a warning and the counselor grabbed Ken by the collar, lifted him from the ground, and hauled him off to isolation.

This time the assistant superintendent, Charles Alexander, talked with Ken.

"I think we'll just leave you here for a while. At least we know where you are, and you can't hit any of the staff with shovels."

"Look, man, I'll mellow it. This is kind of a drag in here. If you let me out I won't hit anybody with shovels." So Mr. Alexander agreed to put Ken back in the group. Of course the boy hadn't said he wouldn't cut out, and the next day he did.

"I split from the rec hall through the back door and across the field. I wasn't in as good a shape as I thought I was, so I got caught. Everybody was after me—counselors and boys."

Another counselor, Mike Martin, again tried talking with Kenny. "If you get your head together, you can make it through this program. You really ought to try."

Ken's response was to bet with Pete, one of his partners from the outside then at the ranch, and make plans for the next escape.

"This time, Pete," Ken suggested, "let's take along some pool sticks. If any of those A boys come after us, we've got a handy, light weapon we can use."

But Pete wasn't anxious to go, so Ken waited until the next night. The nightwatchman came across Ken in the dorm getting his clothes on and asked, "Where are you going?"

"I'm leaving, man. I'm going home. I've had it with this place."

The commotion aroused the other boys, and before long a whole group of them surrounded Ken and once again he was in isolation. He found it hard to understand how the other boys would step in to a situation and help a counselor keep another boy from running away, or catch one who did split. But it happened regularly.

This particular night was especially bad. Ken was violent, lockers were knocked over, and there was a wild melee before Kenny was once again locked up. The incident was the talk of the ranch.

These incidents were my first introduction to Ken as I was ministering to the boys at the ranch. We had weekly, voluntary Campus Life meetings with the guys where we shared the Christian faith as a basis of successful living. We had seen a number of the boys come to know the Lord and their lives really changed out of that experience.

But Kenny was neither an attender at our club meetings nor even open to any of our Campus Life workers.

He made it quite clear he had no time for us, our Bible, or our faith in Jesus Christ. "Preacher, lay off me with that God stuff. That's one disease I don't want to catch," he replied one night when I invited him to a club meeting.

Frankly I was thoroughly convinced the ranch was wasting its resources on a young man who had no intentions of changing. When the question of what to do with him came up, and it did rather regularly, I was firmly on the side of getting rid of him. "If he wants to go to the Youth Authority, he ought to have the opportunity," I told the superintendent.

I recall telling another counselor, "It's a shame Alcatraz is closed. For Ken Pestana, they should reopen it." I was only half joking.

By mutual agreement Ken and I kept a good distance from each other.

But his counselor, Ben Duarte, thought otherwise, and I might add that he was almost alone in his defense of Ken. More than once Mr. Duarte told me there was good potential in Ken that would some day come out.

"Don't try to tell me that," I told him. "Go convince Ken and good luck. You'll need it. I hope you can survive with this kid."

And Mr. Duarte did talk to Ken.

"Ken, I don't know what it is with you. I know something inside of you can make it, but you don't want to make it. What's wrong with you?"

Ken's response at first was to call the man every foul name in the book. "If I ever see you on the streets when I get out of here, I'm going to kill you! Count on that. I hate your guts."

Mr. Duarte was human enough to get angry, and Ken kept hoping the counselor would strike the first blow, but he never did. Ken kept trying to provoke his counselor into a rash action that the boy could use to justify his own belligerence. The tactic didn't work.

The priest also talked to Ken. He gave Ken a small cross and said, "Let's talk about your problems. You do have problems, don't you?"

"Yeah, I got problems. You're here. That's one of them."

The priest offered Ken a Bible and invited him to express his feelings.

"Okay, you want to know how I feel. I don't dig your lousy God, your lousy Bible, your lousy Jesus Christ, your whole lousy religious trip. Just get away from me with that whole mess. I don't need it."

"Why are you so violent, so filled with hate?" the priest asked.

"Why don't you just split and leave me alone? Take that cross and give it to somebody else."

"I'm going to leave this Bible with you."

"Hey, I don't want it."

"Well, I'm going to leave it anyway."

"Get out of my room, sucker!" Ken finally shouted, concluding the interview.

The man of God, discouraged, got up, left the Bible and walked out.

Ken's response to the Word of God was to go through page after page and scribble every vulgar, profane thought he could think of on its pages.

Mr. Duarte saw what was happening and said, "Kenny, that's a crude thing to do. That's a sacred, spiritual message on those pages. If you don't accept it, you don't have to try to destroy it."

"I don't need that book. I told the priest I'd destroy the book if he left it here. I don't need McLean, that priest, or anybody else telling me about God."

That was not the end. There was more to come.

During another escape attempt he attacked Mr. Martin with a pipe he had smuggled into the dorm, and only the intervention of his friend Pete and some of the other wards prevented another serious incident.

Ken's circle of friends was rather limited. Enough of the staff had encounters with Ken so that almost to a man they were disgusted with him, and even many of the boys resented Ken's hostility and hard-guy attitude. The pressure was on to give Kenny his way and let him go to the Youth Authority. Ben Duarte decided to try just one more time to break through to his rebellious young counselee.

Ken tells what happened.

"There were a few people that brought me around an awful lot. One was the cook who believed in me and actually got me to the point where I would do anything to keep her trust.

"As for Duarte, there was no way I could get him off my back. He kept coming, kept asking why I was doing what I was doing. He wanted to know how I really felt and what I was thinking.

"One night he said, 'Look, Ken, I know you've been out on the streets. I know you have feelings against your family. I know you resent authority. Sure, the counselors and kids are riding you. You're a setup. They're enjoying it. Do you like to be setup, man?' "

"No, I don't."

" 'Well, then, use your head. The guys are reporting you so they can look better and get themselves out. And you're dumb enough to blow your cool and let them do it. Do you like to see guys walk all over you to get out of here?'

"The only person I want out of here is me," I told him.

" 'They're going to call you a sucker; then when you blow up they'll stay calm, turn you in and score the points. And you're the loser. If you're dumb enough to hit some kid, he'll laugh at you when he's promoted and you're still down the ladder. Smarten up, Kenny, these guys are using you. They're going to be walking out that door and you aren't.' "

That did it. When Kenny understood the situation as it really was he responded. "I decided to work twice as hard as the other guys and I could do it too. I had to show those counselors that I was tough enough to make it through their program. That was the only form of being tough they understood, and if that was the case, I'd beat them at their own game."

When Ken finally turned around it was quite a performance. His grades at school, reports on work detail—in fact, every phase of the program—shot from the bottom to the best in the ranch. In sports he was awarded the trophy as best football player of the year.

Ken was doing the program, gaining confidence, making friends. For the first time in a number of years he was doing well and enjoying it.

His belligerence toward me turned to polite cordiality. "I used to give you and your Christian buddies a real bad time and I'm sorry about that. But I'm making it now and doing it on my own. I don't need God or any other crutch to get by. We can visit together but leave your Bible out of it. I don't need that. I'll make it by myself."

I was genuinely glad to see Kenny showing some good progress. He had come a long way. But would he continue in the right direction when he got out? Only three months after he stopped his rebelling he was released.

Could he really make it on his own?

A far more definite answer to that question than Kenny ever imagined lay ahead.

CHAPTER 3

"Get Ready for the Big Payback"

Like most people who finally leave any form of confinement, Ken graduated from the ranch with good intentions. But that was about as far as it went. He had given considerable thought to working for his release and none to what he would have to do if he was going to make it back home.

His family was glad to see him, but it wasn't long before the old pattern of late hours, dubious companions, and poor attitude set Ken and his parents once again at odds.

School was worse. He lasted two weeks. "I felt as if I was still doing time. The teachers were on my back right off, and the dean told me he'd be keeping an eye on me now that I was back from the ranch. It was like they expected me to blow it," Ken explained.

"With the kids it was a different story. They kinda looked up to me as a big man 'cause I just got out of the ranch. The whole scene was a hassle.

"My younger brother, who had pretty much gotten things his own way while I was gone, now felt I was crowding him and he would call me 'jail-bird' and 'punk hoodlum.'

"My parents tried to clamp down on my hours, my crowd, and even my phone calls. I was seventeen and I didn't dig that trip at all. The neighbors warned their kids to stay away from me. Everything added together all but forced me back to the crowd that got into trouble.

"If that's how everybody felt, then that's how it was going to be. All the people wanted to reject me, so they had better get ready for the big payback. And it soon came."

Before long one of his old partners, Frank, called. "Hey Kenny, my brother and I hit a pad last week and got a $700 stereo, and Joe has got a jewelry store setup that should be worth some real coin. Why don't you come in with us? We all know each other and no one will snitch. What do you say?"

What Ken said was yes, and thirty days after his release from a juvenile rehabilitation center, he was firmly on the wrong road. Only now he was more sophisticated, cynical, and even better educated in the ways of crime.

"The way that ranch program works is like this: If a guy wants to make it, there is plenty of help there for him. If he doesn't want to make good or doesn't have it together strong enough to cut it on the outside, then it's not their fault. And sometimes some of the hassles a guy faces on the streets are more than he can take, so he blows it. A lot of guys have come out of the ranch and made good; others have blown it badly. But I don't blame the ranch for that.

"I learned a lot of good things there, but I learned one very dangerous thing: how to manipulate other people to do what I said and wanted. If you know how to manipulate, then you've got it together. I was a master at it."

If anyone is still inclined to blame all delinquency on the poor kid from the slum home in the ghetto who steals to survive, it's time for second thoughts. There are those kids, but Kenny certainly doesn't qualify as one of them.

For openers, his father is a highly successful contracter heading major firms in three states. It's a business Mr. Pestana built from the ground up, starting as a youth at age sixteen. He has put in long, hard hours and keeps a masterful finger on every phase of his huge and far-flung business operations. He is a man of strong feelings and demands from his workers no less than he puts out himself. When it comes to his wife and four children, Mr. Pestana is a very sensitive and deeply concerned man.

Ironically, Mr. Pestana's great success in business may have contributed to his son's downfall. It's hard for a dad to face this, but Ken's father does. He does not dispute Ken's statement, "My dad was always busy, tired or gone when I needed him."

The pressures and time-demands of heading a huge business empire all but destroyed the relationship between Ken and his father. It took the crushing tragedy of a murder charge to bring the two men together in a way they had not been for years, if ever.

Ken's mother, attractive, charming, loves an active life with her family and in the out-of-doors. She is an avid tennis player and enjoys fishing. It was on her shoulders that the major responsibility for raising Kenny and the other children fell.

As might be expected the family home can only be described as a mansion. It dominates a spacious area of beautiful residential estates in Saratoga. The well-kept lawns and the large swimming pool provide the setting for a wide variety of activities for a very busy family. Ken's mother designed the home, and its elegance is an impressive tribute to her fine sense of beauty and taste.

Several luxury cars are usually parked in the garage, most with telephones to keep Mr. Pestana in touch with his business even on the road. Two airplanes and a full-time pilot stand by to take the family anywhere business or pleasure may demand.

"We're not poor," Ken admits. But the family success and means is not something Ken brags about. All the time I knew Ken at the ranch, he made not the slightest mention of his family's position nor gave even a faint hint of being impressed with the material gain that surrounds him. He insists he has worked for nearly all of the things he has now. On one subject there has always been agreement between Ken and his parents: children should not be handed things; they should work for them. But Ken feels that his folks have lowered the standard with his younger brother. In fact, he feels that all the other children have had it easier than he ever did.

An older sister is married, and Ken's other sister attends a private Christian college. John, Ken's younger brother by four years, is an enthusiastic drummer and quick to remind anyone he is as big as Ken. John would like to say he is as strong as Ken too, but that claim is subject to debate between the two boys. The natural rivalry between the brothers is as intense as it is in most families.

Ken traces his problems back to about the time he started school as a youngster. He remembers putting his fist through a glass door in a row with his sister when he was only six years old.

Perhaps because of emotional problems, certainly not lack of intelligence, Ken was a slow learner at school.

"This was a real issue between my mom and me," Ken states. "I think she wanted to see me as a good student and athlete like so many other kids in the neighborhood. And she kept the pressure on. She had expectations for me, and I was supposed to live up to them. I fought back. Things got worse. Her defense was a whipping; mine was rebellion. The more I felt they wanted me to be like the other rich society people, the more I chose to be the exact opposite.

"I decided no one was going to push me around. My parents molded me into what I am. And I became mean, hateful and tough. My friend Frank had the same hassles. We were two loners in the same boat—a sinking boat. Misery loves company and we were two of a kind. But I have always been the stronger and took the lead. I was filled with bitterness and meanness inside and there was no way to let it out."

Ken's time at school was always unpleasant. Indeed, his classroom experiences would make an interesting study all by themselves. Although he was an intelligent young man, Ken found learning difficult from the beginning. However, he was always promoted to the next grade only to get further behind in his ability to read and comprehend. Coerced by his inadequacy, he became increasingly rebellious and a disciplinary problem.

Then came the bad part: he was evaluated and labelled as incorrigible, with the reports being passed from teacher to teacher. Soon a new teacher would say, "Oh, there's nothing I can do for him." So that teacher wouldn't give him much help anymore. At that point the boy engaged in more and more bizarre behavior, adding to the attention he was getting by just not producing. And the misconduct kept getting more serious.

With both his academic and disciplinary problems building, the next step was to have him removed from the learning environment because he was too disruptive. Now he was deprived of the very opportunity he needed most. At about the fifth grade he was in deep trouble academically and socially, and of course was thoroughly labelled in school files for it. Was anyone really surprised when he was ready to drop out of high school?

Refusing to come to grips with the problems of a student early enough and passing him on from one teacher to the next is an all too familiar pattern, and one can only hope the teachers and administrators who perpetuate the cruelly inept system, along with its destructive labelling of children, will one day be called to account for how they have tragically mishandled young lives.

Ken's parents saw themselves caught in the middle between a problem son and a system frustrated at meeting his needs.

"We wanted very much to prevent the tragedies that happened to Ken," his mother explained. "If we hadn't kept after him to go to school, he wouldn't have gone at all. He would never do his work. I spent many hours talking with school counselors, teachers, and psychiatrists and followed the suggestions they gave me to motivate and interest Ken in doing some good things with the ability and talents he had. I was thinking only of his future and happiness. He didn't need to succeed for us. He should have wanted to make a happy life for himself, and that he chose not to do.

"Yes, I was concerned about his choice of friends. A number of them had as many or more problems than he. I knew there'd be trouble and there was. The combination could only be bad, and I did all I could to discourage it.

"His father was busy and away often and didn't have the natural, relaxed time with Ken a boy needs. But when either of us made an honest, sincere attempt to communicate with Ken, more often than not he wasn't interested. Understanding is a two-way street. Ken shut us out."

Ken accepts that last statement. His choice of friends was poor, and he gave his parents plenty of reason for concern.

At twelve he was smoking marijuana and had started on reds. The dope scene did nothing for his ability to relate and function well. At thirteen he broke into a school and set the administration office on fire. He wasn't caught.

As things got worse his parents in turn became suspicious, concerned, and finally downright angry as various unexplained supplies of money, motorcycle parts, tape decks, shells, knives, and finally drugs and weapons began showing up around their home.

Eventually his parents forced the action that caused Ken to be sent to the ranch. He bitterly resented it, but they felt there was no other choice.

"We either had to turn him in or be a party to his stealing, and that we would not do," Mr. Pestana explained. "We tried everything else we knew first."

"My parents found a gun in my room and they were afraid I might use it," added Ken. "My pal Joey was going to use that gun to commit suicide because his girl friend left him. And I believed he would do it. I took the gun and hid it in my room. And I did intend to keep it. That was the last straw. My people told the court they couldn't handle me, and I went to the ranch."

Ken's folks may have requested he be sent to the ranch, but certainly they did not neglect him once he arrived at Morgan Hill.

"We visited him regularly," Mr. Pestana emphasized, "and often it was a pretty sad experience. With his escapes, fights and rebellion we spent more time with him in the close security of the dormitory than over at the picnic area by the river. It was the most depressing thing you can ever imagine to see your son fighting himself, his parents, the ranch, and seemingly the whole world."

Unfortunately the time at the ranch only delayed Ken's rebellion at home. It did not stop it. Soon after his release, the uncontrollable young gangster-in-the-making teamed up to lead his buddies, and they were going fast and furious down the road to big trouble.

The mother of one of Ken's girl friends didn't like her daughter running around with a young man who dressed, looked, and acted like a hoodlum. Ken's response was to drive by and shoot out a window of the house with a rifle. But this, like many of his escapades, was never reported to the authorities.

A protection racket run by Ken and his pals centered on local students. Around the campus and in the community, students, including many bigger and stronger than Ken, often paid money to Ken and Frank to keep from being hurt. "It was interesting to see those clean-cut types forking over coin for protection," Ken said.

Ken had other ways of getting what he wanted. A liquor store wouldn't sell cigarettes to him because he was not yet eighteen years of age. So he took out a gun and got his cigarettes along with all the cash in the till. There were a number of assaults—some reported, most not.

One Sunday Ken and a couple of his pals "hit" a church just as the service was ending. In the parking lot they cornered the last few people leaving and took a few wallets. Frank was in on that job and grabbed the purse of a lady who steadfastly refused to surrender it.

Later Frank found some bennies and reds in the purse and laughed. "That's those religious people for you," he commented cynically.

"If I was getting uptight, so were the cops. The sheriff's patrol often stopped and searched me, checking for knives or guns. So I never carried a piece in town.

"I was so sick of everything that I just didn't care and consequently did some reckless, dangerous things. One day I pulled out a pocket comb that works like a switchblade and threatened a patrolman who stopped me. He instantly had his gun out and cocked ready to fire. When he saw that he had almost shot a kid just over a comb, he was shaking. He told me how stupid I was and asked what I was trying to prove. I laughed and said, 'Nothing.' "

Ken and his group were a loosely knit gang who referred to themselves informally as the Ball and Chain. They had dreams of rumbles with other groups of guys, hoping to turn San Jose neighborhoods into the streets of New York. They never made it, although there were a few skirmishes.

"Luckily no dudes got blown away, but several came mighty close. Human life was pretty cheap—mine and everybody elses," Ken added.

"One day an unfriendly rival was driving through what we considered our turf. My partner Frank got excited and urged me to shoot the punk. I reached into my vest and got out a .22 pistol. I was ready to fire; then I laughed and holstered my piece.

"Frank asked, 'What's wrong with you?'

"I told him nothing was wrong. I just didn't

want to waste a shell on him.

"Some of our coin came from an interest we had in the local student dope business, a cut on sales made in our area. That was an easy take 'cause no junkie we ripped off would snitch us to the law."

Perhaps that policeman had asked a more important question than he realized. What *was* Ken trying to prove?

"I'll tell you. I wanted to be the biggest, the top. I wanted to run everything if I could. This was something that had built up for a long time. It was my buddies and me against everybody else. That's the way it was and that's how we played it."

The Christmas season only stepped up their activities.

Ken and Al broke into a home Christmas Eve and stole all the family presents under the tree. They scrawled a note on the mirror, "Scrooge and the Grinch were here."

"At the time, I thought it was very funny," Ken stated. "Actually it was one of the sickest things we ever did."

Back at his uncle's house, which he was watching while the family was away, Ken sat down with Marilyn to size up his Christmas.

"Hey Ken, I've got something for you," Marilyn volunteered.

It was 3 T-shirts, a carton of cigarettes, and a candied apple.

Ken laughed. "Al is in the other room. Go wake him up and give him half the cigs and the candied apple."

Marilyn did what she was told. A few minutes

later Al called to Ken.

"Hey, man, this ain't much, but it's the first gift anybody gave me in a couple of years." He seemed genuinely appreciative.

But depression soon dominated the unhappy trio again.

"This is a lousy Christmas," said Ken.

"Yeah," agreed Al. "What do they even have the holiday for? What does it mean?"

"I don't know," responded Ken.

"Well maybe we can liven up things before New Year's," Al offered. Soon he would take the lead with some big action in mind. Three days later Al, Ken, and Slim were in jail charged with murder.

CHAPTER 4

"I'm the Young Gangster in Big Trouble"

All jails are depressing. Murder max row is just more so.

Ken quickly realized this when he suddenly found himself thrust into the dismal setting and tight security of a cell block that is closely guarded and carefully watched around the clock. Al and Slim had been placed in juvenile hall, so now Ken was alone. Well—not really alone. He shared the misery of fifteen other men all awaiting trial for taking the life of a fellow human being. It was ironic in that Ken, alone among the group, had killed no one.

But then killing and murder are not synonymous. A person may kill another in self-defense, or a law enforcement officer may take the life of a fleeing, dangerous felon and no crime is committed. In fact under those circumstances the killer may in truth be considered a hero. There have been killings but no murder. The laws allow for that distinction. Even the biblical commandment is correctly translated, "You shall do no murder." Thus in both holy writ and the law of the land there is killing without murder. But there is also murder without killing. The Bible calls it murder when a man hates his brother (1 John 3:15).

According to the civil law, a man may wield no weapon or he may even be absent from the scene of a death and yet be charged and found guilty of first degree murder. No one claimed Ken was in the store, pulled the trigger, or even had a weapon. He was a block away when the young store clerk was tragically killed. But if the state could prove that he was part of, or assisted in, a crime that resulted in death, murder would be the charge. That was Ken's situation.

Ken was not the youngest resident of murder row. That distinction went to a seventeen-year-old boy transferred from juvenile court, charged with strangling his mother and trying to frame his father for the crime. His cell was next to Ken's.

His cellmate during most of the six months Ken was on the row was a very unlikely defendant in a criminal case. But then no crime has more varied types of the accused than murder. Robert, in his forties, a college computer specialist with a brilliant mind, had murdered his wife in a fit of rage. He could hardly remember the details of the terrible tragedy and was filled with remorse for what had been the one violent act of an otherwise unblemished life. Ken and Robert contrasted in age, temperament and in most other respects, but they became good friends.

Ken had plenty of time to rest and think; in fact, he did little else. The only time he left his cell was to appear in court or to see his attorneys, his parents, or me. On those occasions he was first stripped and searched, then dressed

Ken and Robert in a murder-max row security cell.

in an orange surplus paratroop jump suit, handcuffed to a chain around his waist and finally shackled at the feet. It was hard to imagine which was worse—the restraint in movement or the humiliation. However, several escape attempts from the row convinced the sherriff that such precautions on all murder suspects were both wise and necessary.

The first person to see Ken following his arrest was his dad's business attorney and longtime family friend, Russell Roessler. He was soon joined by a criminal trial specialist, Angelo Pestarino, who would take charge of the defense.

"I didn't know how to take those guys," Ken commented. "I was impressed that my dad had sent them to represent me, but I didn't know who I could trust. Most of the guys on the row said their lawyers had messed their clients over and sold them out to the district attorney, and I didn't know who to believe. I didn't open up much to those men at first."

Eventually Ken made the wise deduction that jail house lawyers in the cell blocks are not the best source of advice, and he began to confide frankly in the attorneys who had come to help him.

"I remember seeing a lot of lawyers on television," Ken further explained. "They make big emotional speeches to witnesses and the jury and win by pulling some surprise out of the hat at the last minute. The TV lawyers are either emotional wizards or slick operators. My attorneys didn't seem like that."

Indeed they were not. Mr. Roessler brought

to the case the solid confidence of Ken's father and a wealth of contacts and experience in local law enforcement circles, having represented the police and sheriffs' associations for many years.

As for Mr. Pestarino, he is on, if not at the top, of the list of the three or four best criminal attorneys in the whole area. He can afford to be selective about which clients he takes, and he is. A lawyer can handle just so many major cases. But those clients accepted by Mr. Pestarino know they are getting the

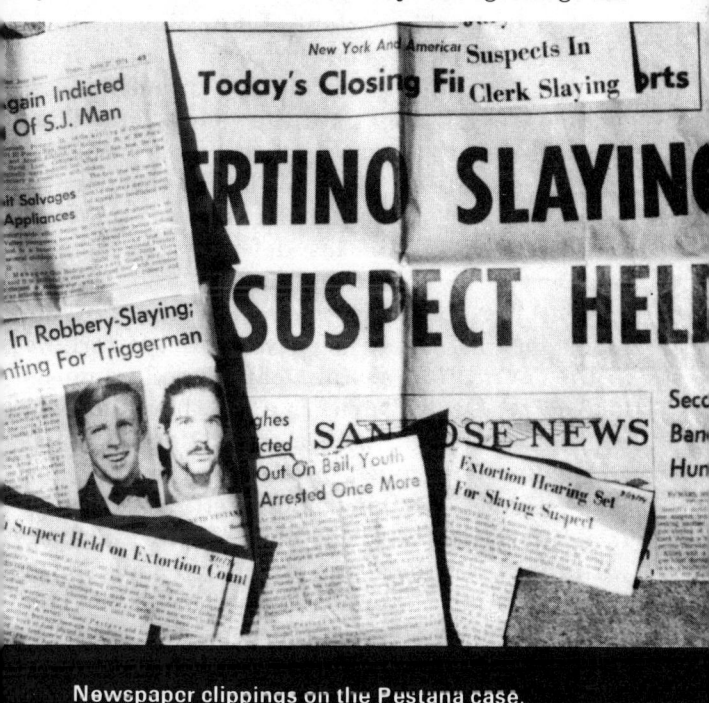

Newspaper clippings on the Pestana case.

service of a highly competent and reputable professional who will work diligently and well in their defense.

A fatherly, distinguished looking man who has been in the prosecutor's office, Angelo Pestarino is friendly, pleasant and inspires a degree of confidence in a courtroom that has to be seen to be fully appreciated. Judges and jurors instinctively like and trust him. However, behind that casual manner is an alert mind, a thorough knowledge of the law, and a detailed grasp of the case he is presenting.

Ken had an important thing going for him: Mr. Pestarino, a good judge of people from years of listening to all manner of defendants, instantly and deeply liked the young man. That measure of trust was at times badly shaken along the route to the trial, but it never really waivered. For Ken that feeling was mutual; the more he saw of his defender the greater was the youth's respect.

The prosecutor on the case was one of the most capable young deputy district attorneys in the courts. The son of a church college music instructor, David Davies is a tall, blond-haired, neatly attired man with a reputation for being compellingly thorough in the preparation of his cases. He puts in long hours getting ready for trial and expects the police officers working with him to do the same. He has probably never uttered an idle, unplanned word in his life. He works hard to gain convictions and believes firmly in the authority of the courts to punish those who have transgressed, a position he knows is well received in the community. His personal opinion of Kenny was never likely a factor in Mr. Davie's pursuit of the case. He was there to do a job, and he would do it to the very best of his considerable ability.

Not surprisingly, Ken did not like the tactics the district attorney used and was thoroughly angered at some of the things the man said and did in the courts. But yet Ken respected the prosecutor.

"That guy is good at his job, man," Ken often said. "I have to keep telling myself he genuinely believes I am as bad as he keeps saying. I presume he considers Al worse, but I am not really sure of that. Mr. Davies is a very good attorney, a hard working man. I can see him going home at night and telling his family, 'I sure messed over that bad kid Kenny today.' But that is what he's supposed to do and he does it well. I just wished he worked for my side," he concluded, paying to Mr. Davies what for Kenny was a great tribute.

The superior court judge who presided over most of the proceedings in the case, including the trial and sentencing, was Judge James Duvaras, Jr. Ken came to deeply admire him, not because the judge always ruled in Ken's favor—often he did not—but because Ken saw in the judge a sincere man honestly trying to do what was the right and fair thing.

"No matter what finally happens, that man will give me a fair hearing. He listens carefully to everybody before he makes up his mind, and you can see him up there struggling to find what is right, no matter who it helps or hurts. There is a great man," commented Kenny.

But if Kenny's reactions to the principles in his court actions were calm and objective, his reaction to confinement was not. As the court actions dragged on and the weeks on murder max row turned into months, the patience of the young prisoner wore thin.

Ken now smoked two packs of cigarettes a day. His cell partner bore the brunt of Ken's frustrations. "Many nights guys would take out their tensions by banging on the walls. It was maddening, and I couldn't understand it until one night I almost flipped out myself. I started yelling at my cellmate, swearing at the top of my lungs, asking what kind of an animal would cold bloodedly murder his wife. He just turned away from me and sat down on his bunk. There were tears in his eyes. If he had screamed back or hit me, I would have expected it. But he didn't, and I realized what I had done. Robert had been a good friend, listening to my problems, giving me some good, fatherly advice, and now I had really hurt him.

"I apologized. Up to that time in my life I hadn't done that very often, but I told him I was sorry. I asked him how he managed to keep himself together under the pressure.

" 'I pray, Kenny,' he softly replied.

"You do what?" I asked, half questioning, half laughing.

" 'I ask God to forgive me for what I did and to help me face what is ahead. I still don't know all I need to about getting to Him, but I'm working on it.'

"Now you gotta understand that religion was not a very popular subject on the row. The chaplain and his helpers who came in to hold a service for us each week had to put up with a lot of cat calls, insults, banging cups on bars and flushing toilets. And I was right in there causing a commotion with a rest.

"During a service I called out to the kid in the next cell, 'Check out that preacher's suit. What do you think it's worth?'

"He called back, 'About two bucks, probably bought it at the flea market.'

"But the people holding the meeting never got angry. They would just smile, hand us some Christian leaflets or magazines, offer to pray for us and leave. It was maddening. We were acting like fools, and they were all calm and polite.

"To make things worse the chaplain regularly stopped at my cell to talk, asked me how things were going, and if there was anything he could do to help. At first I was just rude or sent him on, but soon the situation got downright embarrassing. The guy kept coming back and I started being halfway decent to him.

"It was at one of those visits I asked if he could have Mr. McLean come up and see me. He came and visited several times, mainly renewing an old friendship, if you can call it that, from my days at the ranch. The best thing about those visits was the opportunity to get out of my cell for a while, and I was willing to listen to him talk about God for that change of pace.

"I didn't attempt to fool Mr. McLean about any serious religious intentions on my part. We knew each other too long and too well for that."

"You know, I think those church people really like you," his cellmate told Ken one day.

"I sure can't figure out why," Ken responded. "I don't like to listen to them, and everything they give me to read I tear up. I used to do it right in front of them; now I've improved—I wait till they leave."

But one day he didn't tear up the literature, and Robert said, "Sit down, Ken, I'm going to read some of this to you." Surprisingly Ken made no objection. After reading the gospel tract, Robert read some from the Bible while again Ken listened. Then Robert started to pray.

"Why do you do that?" Ken interrupted. "He can't hear you, whispering here in a cell."

"But He does hear me," Robert responded.

"How do you know He does?"

"Since I started praying, I've been able to sleep at night," was the quiet, firm reply.

Ken was stunned, and mockingly put on a show. He laughed and then jumped up on his bunk. But soon he started to pray—in whispers, so no one would know he was doing it. At last Kenny was talking to God. "Wherever you are, God, listen to me. You know me. I'm the young gangster in big trouble. I'm sick and tired of who I am and what I am doing. My mind is going crazy. I was in on a terrible job where a young guy, who never hurt anyone and who I never knew, got blown away. I'm hurting my parents. I'm miserable with my partner here. I even give people working for You a bad time. It's all got to stop, God, and I don't know how to do it or even where to begin. Will You show me?"

Ken's cell partner on murder-max row helps him to read. Their lesson material, *The Way*.

Ken was right about the pressures. They were getting to him. It hurt both him and his parents to look out through a thick glass in the visiting room with him shackled and talking over a telephone.

He had even thought of killing himself. On the way to court one day, he considered grabbing one of the guns his guard had in an open holster. At the last minute he decided against it, not because it was wrong, but because just as he was about to make his move several other deputy sherriffs happened along. Shackled as he was at that time, it would have been suicide.

Oddly enough while bail had been set for Al at $100,000, the court had steadfastly refused to even consider bail for Ken. For six months he had been on murder max row, and one day he jokingly suggested to Pestarino, "Why don't we go for bail again?" The attorney agreed it was a good idea and said he would schedule the court session.

Ken couldn't believe it; he had only been kidding.

That night he had a second, long talk with God that lasted several hours.

Ken recalls the major things he said. "God, I hope You're listening. I don't think You owe me any favors, but please don't be mad if I ask for one. I've got to see my family again. If I don't get out, please help me go through what is ahead 'cause right now I am alone and scared.

"I don't know how to trust You, God. I've burned a lot of people, and You know how many have burned me. I feel like an old man. I'm

18 going on 100.

"But I'll tell You this. I've got to have some assurance You're there and You care. If You let me out for a while, I'll accept You into my life. I'll find Your way, and my life is all Yours. You can do with me whatever You want.

"God, I know You don't make deals with people. I either come on Your terms or not at all. I get that message loud and clear. But let me out of this hole for a while. I'll get my head cleared up, and You'll have one faithful guy on Your team."

Ken was speaking pretty loud and his cellmate heard him.

"That's no good, Kenny. If you're going to come to God, it has to be whether you get out or not."

"God, he's right," Ken continued. "I guess I want out so bad I'm getting some things mixed up. God, I want to find You. Please send somebody to help me. If it's not at home, then in here."

For the first time in six months Kenny genuinely felt the load was lighter. That night he had a good sleep.

A few days later the court assembled to hear the request for bail. The district attorney vigorously opposed any bail because of the serious crime charged, but Kenny's attorneys argued that bail was a right that every defendant should have prior to trial. Bail should never, in their opinion, be a form of pretrial punishment.

The judge ruled that Kenny could have bail, but the figure set for it was enormous. Ken's parents had to post a $200,000 property bond so their son could come home.

There were some conditions. Ken had to be in every night at 9 unless he was with his parents. That order was later amended to include his activities with Campus Life. He was expected to work for his father and of course make all court appearances.

Late that night when the paperwork was completed, Ken was released and went out for a meal with his mother. The restaurant, quiet and practically deserted at the late hour, was such a contrast to the constant banging and noise of max row that it was difficult for Kenny to adjust.

He knew he would undoubtedly go in lockup again after the trial, but that night the fresh breeze and the quiet streets were the most beautiful things he could imagine. Tonight he would sleep in his own bed again. To most guys that was no big thing. To him it would be pure luxury. For the moment he was free and that's all that mattered.

As they drove home little did Ken and his mother realize that just ahead lay a crisis that was suddenly to land him back in jail, threaten his whole defense, and cause his family and friends to panic.

There was also some unfinished business to take care of with God.

CHAPTER 5

"God, You and Me Are So Far Apart"

It was good to be home. However, the happiness at getting out of jail and the pleasure of seeing his family didn't solve all of Ken's problems. He agreed not to see his old partners, but that was easier said than done. When word of his release spread, the old crowd was on the phone, stopping by the house, or running into Ken around town.

One such casual meeting sparked a new nightmare. Ken was having coffee at a restaurant with two girls he knew only slightly when Bill, a fellow graduate of the boys' ranch, stopped to rap. The subject came up concerning a contract that Frank, one of Ken's friends, had out on Bill's life. Bill believed Frank wanted him hurt or killed, and Kenny did nothing to relieve the young man's worry. Quite the contrary.

"Yeah, that's so. Frank wants you all right. But I think you can buy him off. He probably wants $100 but he may take less. Tell you what I'll do. Give me forty bucks and I'll talk to him for you and see if I can get him to take the money and lay off you."

Bill wasn't prepared to pay on the spot, so the matter was dropped. Ken quickly forgot the incident.

A few days later I returned from a speaking tour and stopped by the county jail to see Ken, whom I had not visited for several weeks. I was informed he had been released on bail. I told the jailer I didn't really believe Ken would get out.

"We didn't either," he pointedly responded, indicating anything but pleasure at Ken's return to the community, even for a short period of time.

A few hours later I phoned Ken and he told me about his getting out and suggested I come by the house. I was pleased at the warmth of his response and agreed to meet him that night.

He was much more relaxed sitting and visiting in the recreation room of his home than he had ever been shackled and talking across the table in the small jail counseling room. He was friendly, responsive, and I could see we were going to get along well. I brought him a copy of *The Way*, the Living Bible, and no longer did he cast it aside with a snide remark. I was now confronted by a very sober, thoughtful young man who had obviously been through a very trying ordeal that was still far from over. He appeared to have matured a good deal in the crisis. The visit was good and we agreed to continue meeting on a regular basis.

One week later Bill phoned Kenny, anxious to arrange an in-person meeting. Bill felt that Frank was still after him. "Look, Ken," he offered, "I've got $45 and 40 reds. I want to pay off the contract that is out on me."

"Frank is *your* man," Ken replied. "I have nothing really to do with this; it's not my trip,

I'm not involved, I didn't make any contract. I'll see if I can get hold of Frank and let you know. I don't want to see you get hurt, that's all. I told Frank he was crazy. He got mad at some guy last week and threw him off a dam. That's a crazy thing to do for kicks. I can't see that. He gets off work soon. I'll try to get hold of him now and tell him what you want. Call me back in a few minutes."

Shortly after, Bill again placed a call to Ken.

"Frank doesn't want any reds, just some money," Ken reported. "He'll take $45 down and the rest later. I'll pass it on to him for you. If you've got $75 that's better. You owe him $100. It's all right if you bring over $75 now; $75 will cut it."

"I can't come now," Bill pleaded. "I've got to be to work in ten minutes and my mother is going to drive me. I'll have to make it later. I can meet you when I get off."

"Hey," said Ken, "you can't work if you're gone for good. If you can't bring it now, go by a telegraph office and wire it to me on your way to work. I'll get it to Frank. Then I won't be afraid of your burning Frank or Frank burning you."

Bill asked for more time and said he'd call again.

That night Ken told me about the calls, mentioning that the sheriff's officers had talked with him about his initial encounter with Bill, adding that he didn't know what to make of the whole affair.

I was angry. "Look Ken, this is nothing but trouble. You don't need to get in the middle of any feud between Frank and Bill. You're out on bail for murder, and if Bill gets hurt you'll be the first guy they'll come and see. You can't afford to be in on anything that even looks suspicious. Why don't you quit trying to play the big, bad role and get out of these things?"

"Hey, Gordy, I was only trying to keep Bill from being hurt. You know Frank would do it if he said it. And he said it. Pete can tell you that."

"All of that is fine, but you stay out of it. If Bill calls again tell him you want no part of any money, reds, or anything else. Don't meet him, get him off the phone, don't get involved. And then we'll report this whole business to the sheriff's office. Okay?"

Ken agreed.

Five days later Bill placed a third phone call to Ken. This time Bill was anxious to meet Kenny that same night, but Ken followed instructions and said he wanted no part of the problem, would handle no money, and told Bill not to call again. Ken's father came on the phone at the end of the call and also told Bill never again to call the house.

I was told of the conversation and agreed that Ken had at last handled the matter correctly. I told him we would go down together to inform the sheriff's officers of what happened. We did report it. The detective asked Ken a few questions but really didn't seem to be impressed by the whole matter. Furthermore, he didn't appear to put much credence in Bill's fears and tended to confirm my own belief that Bill had an overly vivid imagination.

Ken and I left the detective bureau convinced that the matter was over. We notified his attorneys and they agreed we had done the right thing. Little did we know a time bomb was waiting to explode in the form of a surprising new charge based on Ken's contacts with Bill.

Meanwhile my regular visits with Ken were bringing out into the open many of his problems. He appreciated my interest and I responded to his honest, sensible approach to his needs. Finally he was being realistic. No longer was the subject of the Lord off limits. Far from it.

"Gordy, when I was in jail I told God I wanted out of that cell even for a short time. I didn't really have any right to ask Him for that, but I did and He heard me. I told Him I wanted to change all the sick things I was doing. I want to find Christ, and you're the man He sent to help me do it!"

I couldn't imagine a clearer invitation to present my faith in Christ to a guy, and so we talked about God and man at the turning point in life.

"It wasn't easy up in murder max row," Ken told me. "I worried about what the guys there would think. Me praying—a young tough with one of the biggest beefs on the row. They'd think I was some kind of a sissy. But I prayed anyway, and for the first time I felt at peace with myself. All the bitterness I had been storing up inside started coming out.

"I remember my attitude with you and the Campus Life people who talked with me at the ranch. It was bad. And there was the priest and then the chaplain at the jail who kept coming to see me no matter how much I bad-mouthed him trying to impress the other inmates.

"My cell partner didn't laugh. He was a good man. He had a real respect for God, and helped me with my reading. I kept thinking that the Lord was nothing but a big put-down. I wanted excitement; you know what I mean? The only thing I ever said to the Lord was 'God, You and me are so far apart.' When I told the chaplain that, he just smiled and asked, 'Whose fault is that, Ken?'

"As I look back, there were a lot of things to get me started talking about God."

He told me about a number of them. When he was hitchhiking around the area he would occasionally be given a ride by a Christian anxious to share a witness for his faith. "People would tell me about God and what He meant to them. Sometimes I'd just say, 'Listen, you can take your Jesus stuff and cram it. Let me off right here.' But other times I needed a ride bad enough so I listened. I tried to shut out of my mind what people said about how they loved the Lord and what He had done for them. But that talk ain't easy to forget," Ken commented.

Another time Ken and Frank were broke and tired; the previous three days had been spent in the streets. The pair approached a woman at a shopping center and Ken made her an offer.

"Lady, we ain't going to hurt you. Just listen. I got this tape deck here and I'll let you cop it for some money so we can buy some grub.

We haven't eaten much in a couple of days. What'd you say?"

She said no. But then she came back with a suggestion that must have startled the two young men standing there in dark vests, old T-shirts, greasy jeans, and black gangster brims, looking for all the world like a couple of Hell's Angels.

"I don't want your tape deck and I can't afford to give you any money. But how would you like to come to our apartment with my husband and me, and I'll make you dinner?"

Before the stunned pair could respond, she continued. "There is one condition you need to know. Are you familiar with the Bible? We share a reading from the Bible after dinner each night, and we would want you to join us."

"Wait a minute, lady; now wait a minute," blurted Ken, recovering his speech before Frank did.

"Wait a minute for what, young man?" she replied graciously. "It's only fair to tell you I'm really into Jesus. There's no one in the world that means more to us than Jesus Christ."

The two boys moved a few feet away for a private conversation on how to handle this unexpected turn of events.

"Oh, wow, it's a choice between a free meal with a Bible session or nothing to eat," said Ken.

"Let's split," was Frank's quick verdict. "We can unload the tape deck someplace and get some coin."

"I don't know. My stomach says yes and my mind says no," Ken responded. Frank had no such doubts. "Yeah, well, all of me just says no. What you say we bogey?"

"Look at it this way," Ken reasoned as their prospective host, a few feet away, waited patiently for the decision, "we're going to get a free dinner. We can block out everything they say. I like to rap with these people, you know; lead them on, then tell them what they can do with their Jesus Christ after I eat their nice T-bone steaks. If they get too heavy, we can always tell them we're Satan worshippers. That'd be a total blowout."

"You might have something there," Frank agreed reluctantly. Then he turned to the waiting woman and announced, "After you, lady."

The drive home with the couple in the front seat of their station wagon and the youths in back presented an immediate problem. It began when Frank lit up a joint and offered the couple a hit. It was politely declined.

"That's one thing we're going to have to help you boys with," the lady sweetly suggested. "You just shouldn't get stoned on things like that. If you are going to get stoned, it should only be on Jesus."

"Oh, no," was Frank's dejected response.

"Would you please be so kind as to put that marijuana cigarette out," she politely asked. She repeated her request when Frank wasn't sure he had heard correctly and thanked him when he complied. Ken smiled, fighting hard to keep from openly laughing.

The boys soon learned they had a walk of several floors to the small apartment where the couple, newlyweds, lived.

On the way up the stairs Ken whispered quietly to Frank that they ought to ask the couple for sleeping quarters for the night. "That'll give us a good chance to check out their pad." Frank's business was ripping off people, and he never let good opportunities get far from his thoughts, so he appreciated Ken's sudden inspiration. "Yeah, right on," he whispered back.

At dinner the young couple explained that they had met in church and were very devoted to the Lord and each other. The husband suggested, "You boys wouldn't have to be out on the streets selling tape decks to survive if you knew the Lord. You know the Lord provides for the needs of His people."

Ken opened his vest, patted his holster and gun, and answered, "For me, this provides."

The man looked a little startled. "Is that a real gun?"

Ken nodded. "Sure is."

"Is it loaded?" asked their host, still not showing much emotion.

Again Ken nodded in the affirmative.

"Now, we can't have that in our home," the man explained kindly. "Would you please set it down somewhere. A loaded gun just doesn't go well with good fellowship and Bible study around the table."

"I don't let my piece out of my sight," Ken countered.

"Me neither," seconded Frank, showing his weapon.

The man turned calmly to his wife. "I can just see we're going to have to have a serious talk with these boys. This will never do, dear."

"By the way," asked the wife, hoping to ease the tension, "You mentioned you have several tape decks. Where do you get your supply?"

Ken almost choked on his meat before answering. "Well, you see it's like this. You might say there are a few places we know where we can get them rather quickly with very little hassle."

That subject, too, was quickly dropped.

Then came a talk about the Lord that lasted until the early morning hours. It was pretty one-sided. The boys were much too tired to argue and decided to simply agree with everything the couple said.

Suddenly the lady turned to Frank. "I believe the Spirit of God is dealing with you, young man."

"He is?" replied the startled youth, suddenly wide awake.

"He can come into your life and change it right now," her husband added enthusiastically.

"Not if I don't want it to happen," an uncomfortable Frank replied, not used to being on the defensive.

"Quite true," said the lady. "You know, I think you boys have come a long ways tonight."

"If you think we've done well tonight, we might come even further tomorrow if you let us sleep in your pad," eagerly suggested Ken while his partner turned to survey the stereo and figure out how to get it out of the apartment and down the stairs.

The couple agreed with Ken and got some

sleeping bags for the pair. As soon as the bags were in place the lady suggested, "Of course we'll all have to say a prayer before we go to sleep."

"Prayer?" queried Frank. "Look, lady, I don't know how to do that."

"Well you can start by folding your hands," the lady kindly offered.

"What was that?" asked Frank.

"Fold your hands."

The boys complied.

"Would you like to say a prayer or would you like us to?" asked the lady.

"You! by all means you!" said the startled pair almost in unison.

She did and when the boys were finally alone, they analyzed their predicament.

"This is bad news," volunteered Ken. "We'd better get out of here first thing tomorrow."

"I think you got a good idea there," Frank readily agreed. With that both boys went to sleep, their guns within easy reach.

The next morning at breakfast the couple offered to let the boys stay on for a few days.

"Well, uh, I'm sure sorry, we'd like to, but, well, we've got some business we got to take care of," Ken answered, searching for words.

"Yeah, important business," added Frank.

"Oh that's too bad," replied the lady, real regret in her words. "And we were just getting to know you, and God was getting His love through to you."

"Yeah, you don't know how hard it is to leave with all that happening," responded Ken, trying to keep a straight face. "By the way, can we borrow five dollars?"

Ken expected a hassle on that but was surprised by the woman's quick agreement as she reached for her purse.

"I mean I just can't take your money. It's gonna be a loan or something," Ken offered.

"Take it, Ken, just take it," whispered Frank.

"No," said Ken, "we've got to work this out."

"All right," suggested the lady. "Leave your tape deck here and when you come to pay back the five dollars, I'll return it to you."

"Fair enough," said Ken and the boys got their five dollars and left. They had no plans to return.

On the way down the street Frank laughed hilariously at their experience, but Ken wasn't quite so flippant.

"You know, Frank, those people wouldn't do what they're doing if they didn't have joy, real love, and God in their lives. They either are nutty and belong in a mental hospital or they're right in what they say," he reasoned.

"Come on, Ken, forget it. It's all over. It was just a bad nightmare."

"Maybe, but I'll tell you one thing, Frank, say what you want, those people are a lot happier than we are."

CHAPTER 6

"You're Not the Guy
I Used to Know"

"There's something important we got to talk about tonight," Ken said, greeting me one evening as I arrived at his home.

"What have you done now?" I asked cautiously.

"No, it's nothin' like that. I'm cooling it," responded Ken as we relaxed in the rec room.

"Like I told you before, when I was in jail I told God I wanted to get it right with Him and get a lot of things goin' on the inside of me straightened out. It's buggin' me that I really haven't taken care of that yet. Let's nail it down. What do you say?"

"Okay, Ken," I replied. "Just why do you want to get it together with the Lord? You and I both know people around town will say you're faking it, hoping to have God get you off in court or something."

"That's crazy, man, real crazy. I got into this mess, and neither God nor anybody else is getting me out of it. I need to get myself straightened out and then get some strength to face all that will happen in court and when I go to the joint. And you and I both know I'm gonna do time. God isn't going to get me out of that. What I hope is that He'll help me go through it and not come out more mixed up and worse than I've been. Do you read me?"

I got the message very clearly. Ken may have played games with many people, but he never tried it with me. Good or bad, and most of the time previously it had been bad, he had been frank in our relationship. Often I didn't like what he told me, but at least I knew I was getting what he honestly felt. He wasn't trying to use God or squirm out of his problems. He was sincerely looking for a way through them.

"Just how does this Jesus Christ deal work?" he asked.

"A guy has to begin by admitting he's blown it badly with God," I responded. "You know, most of us are in the habit of blaming other people, circumstances, raw deals, anybody or anything but ourselves for the mess our life gets in."

Agreeing, Ken noted, "I read some books with big fancy words to explain why people do what they do: personality disorder, frustrations, all that kind of stuff."

"Ken, those problems are there and they need to be dealt with by people skilled in counseling. But only God can change a guy inside, make him new and start him on the way to life forever with Him."

"Go ahead. That's what I want to get filled in on."

"Look at it this way. Ken, you like to drive, don't you?"

"Do I like to drive?" he responded enthusiastically. "I got the neatest ride in the turf, and you know how I love wheels."

"Are you a good driver, Ken?"

"Oh come on, you know I can handle anything going down," Kenny declared.

"I'm not talking about your car, Ken. I'm talking about your life. For the last eighteen years you've been driving a guy called Ken, figuring where you would go and how fast. I think you missed it, and the Bible says you have. You've made some wrong turns, hit the ditch a few times, and to make matters worse, you've been on the wrong road."

Ken knew that was true and responded, "That's about as far off as a guy can get. I know I've blown it—the night of the robbery and a lot of other times. It's kind of like I had the devil at the wheel steering my life."

"That's pretty close to the truth, Ken, and that's what the Bible means when it says we've all done things to displease God, missed the mark He set for us. But the exciting news is that when we were all mixed up—in fact, even before we were born—God did something to solve the problem for each of us."

"That's pretty heavy, man. That's where Jesus comes in, isn't it?"

"Right, Ken. When God sent His Son to this planet nearly two thousand years ago, He didn't get much of a welcome. There was no room at the Bethlehem Holiday Inn—just a stable out back where Christ could be born."

"What a place to make the scene," Ken added seriously.

"Right you are," I smiled. "Nobody paid

much attention to Christ at first. The people at the inn were too busy at their party to give any thought to God. Things haven't changed too much today on that score."

Ken agreed.

"Two kinds of people came to see that little child: A few wise men who followed a star, and some shepherds who were interrupted by a choir of angels and invited to the manger."

"That's sort of like a television spectacular without the TV," Ken decided.

"But there's more to this," I continued. "Think for a minute. Two kinds of people got to Christ: wise men smart enough to know they didn't know everything and ordinary guys who went looking. They found the Lord. And you know, Ken, the same two kinds of people find Him today."

Ken nodded for me to go on.

"Jesus taught many fine things about how we ought to get along with God, ourselves, and other people. You can read them in your copy of *The Way*. But He did something far more than teach: He died on a cross. And Ken, He had it rough. He was betrayed by a friend, sold out for thirty pieces of silver to a rigged court, passed off by one judge who was a coward and convicted by another who stated publicly that He had done nothing wrong. Then he was dragged through the streets and beaten, made to carry His own cross and finally hung up to die. Even then another condemned man joined the crowd in yelling for Him to come down from the cross."

"Well, why didn't He come down?" Ken

asked.

"Because He had come to die, Ken. God had planned that Christ would give His life for our sins, for the things we've done wrong. Then God would accept Christ's death in our place, so that by coming to Him we could be forgiven."

"Easter is the time when He busted out of the grave, isn't it?"

"Right, Ken. And when Christ came back to life, He proved that everything He claimed, offered, and taught was absolutely true. More important, He said that people who believed in Him could some day do the same thing—come back to life and never again die."

"But how does this get to me?" Ken queried.

"There's been some big battles going on inside you, right?"

"You can say that again," Ken agreed.

"That isn't just your conscience. That is the Holy Spirit of God showing you your need, seeking to bring you to Christ. And when you do accept Him, God's Spirit comes into your life, puts God's life inside you, forgives you, and makes you a child of His."

"But God doesn't force His way in, does He?"

"You know that, Ken. He's been patiently waiting for you for a long time. God may allow a man to come to the end of himself, but the choice of accepting His answer is up to each one of us."

"How do you do it?"

"Look at it this way. A while ago we mentioned you were at the wheel—"

"Or the devil was," Ken interrupted ruefully.

"Okay. But you can change that. You can turn the steering wheel of your life over to the Lord, asking Him to guide and direct you. It's simple but it's not easy. You've really got to want the Lord in your life, really want to change and give Him the right to tell you what to do and how to live."

"Well, just about anything would be an improvement," Ken sighed.

"If you mean that, Kenny, then let's pray."

Frankly, I have never understood the divine chemistry of salvation that allows a broken man to say a prayer of commitment and ask forgiveness, and then come out of that experience transformed and started in a whole new direction in life. But I've seen it often enough to know it works, and that summer night in Ken's home it happened to him.

We shook hands and Kenny talked to God. A few hours later I wrote down what Ken said. I wanted to remember it:

"God, this is Kenny. I'm not used to talking to You yet, but I'm gonna be. I've done some bad, mean things in my life, and You know all about them. About the worst is when I drove a guy to that store and the young fellow in the store got blown away. I can't get that out of my mind. I've done a lot of terrible stuff to my family, other people I don't even know, and, God, I'm really sick of it. I know I'm going to prison and maybe for a long time. I'm not asking You to change that. I got myself into it, and I'll have to go through with it. But I want You to come into my life, forgive me for all I've done that's so bad, and help me to be a good man on Your team. I'll do what You want me to do. And God, when I do get locked up again, give me the strength I need to do the right thing. That's all—except I really mean it. And thank You. Amen."

That was the beginning. A young man had come to the turning point in his life and he had made the right choice.

However, he still had to face all the problems in the courts, and there were more coming that we didn't as yet even know about.

Ken also had inward problems like forgiveness. It is one thing to ask God's forgiveness; it is another for a man to forgive himself. Far from the cold, calculating hood many thought him to be, Ken was a guilt-ridden young man filled with deep remorse over having any part in the tragic killing of the young clerk. He had read a good deal about the youth and even kept a newspaper picture of the boy in his room. While there was no way I wanted him to forget the tragedy, yet I believed Ken had to come to some terms with himself over what had taken place. That kind of emotional healing takes time.

The ideal situation would be to find a Christian friend for Ken, one who was about his own age, strong in the faith, and yet having been in trouble himself so he could relate to the particular pressures Ken was under. That was a big order to find in one person, but there was such a young man available. Sam Free became a friend to Ken and at just the right time.

Sam was out on bail for his participation in the robbery of the home of a prominent local restaurant owner. Sam and an older man, who set up the job, broke into the victim's home, tied up his wife and daughter at gun and knife point, and forced them later to open the safe. They stole cash, jewelry, and valuables and then loaded them into the victim's car, which they also took. The police had the older robber under surveillance, so an arrest was made when the stolen goods showed up at the man's house. Shortly after, Sam also was caught.

Sam had never been in trouble before, adult or juvenile, but for a beginner he had certainly gone about all the way. He faced ten felony charges and was possibly headed for prison.

He is not the kind of young man you associate with trouble. He is handsome, neatly attired, polite, quite unsympathetic to hoods and their attitude, language or dress. He had a strong church background, which he eventually rebelled against after completing high school and deciding to go out on his own. What he found were frustrations, a bad crowd, and plenty of trouble.

But what Sam had learned about God had not been forgotten. And in the holding cell just after his arrest, he got down on his knees and asked God to forgive him and make things right in his life. He didn't need anyone to tell him how. Sam knew the way and the Bible verses better than most people. It was then he decided to apply them to his life instead of merely going through a religious role in a busy church program.

I went to see Sam in custody and often talked with Kenny at the same time. We helped Sam's family secure an attorney and joined in a request for bail so he could be released.

That was a frustrating experience. Everytime we went to court to ask for bail, the judge would raise the required amount. The figure went from $10,000 to $25,000 and finally $50,000. Sam was really upset.

"I told God He wasn't doing me any good at all. But I think He wanted me to know He was making the decisions, not me. It was a good lesson on His authority and taught me some much-needed patience."

Finally on the fourth try the situation was reversed—bail was lowered to $10,000 and Sam was released to his family. He became very active in our Campus Life ministry and his church, showing an enthusiasm and dedication that was contagious. The court actions in his case went on for months, and he had plenty of time to build his own faith and share with many other young people.

He was delighted to meet Ken and was more than eager to fellowship with another fellow going through the courts. Ken's sister Linda didn't seem to mind Sam being around their family home either. Sam and the Pestanas became good friends.

Ken and Sam went to church together, encouraged each other, and shared what they had been reading in *The Way*. In fact, it is a good thing Sam was with Ken at church. One Sunday a police officer who patrols Sam's church to prevent vandalism and theft around the large grounds stopped Ken and wanted to know what the youth was doing there.

"I'm going to the service," Ken replied.

The officer gave him a look that indicated disbelief. It seemed as if the patrolman were saying, "Ken Pestana coming to worship? You've got to be kidding!"

But Sam happened along and explained to the perplexed officer that the infamous Ken Pestana was indeed at church for the right reasons.

Ken told me about the incident and added jokingly, "I've been checked out and almost thrown out of a lot of places before. But this is the first time it happened at church."

However the patrolman's reaction was mild compared to that of Ken's old partners. He met his girl friend one afternoon at a restaurant. While he was waiting for her, he was thumbing through *The Way*. She arrived, sat down, greeted him, ordered some food, and asked casually what the book was all about.

"It's the Bible, " Ken explained. "I'm really getting into this and it's good. I wanted to show it to you." He went on to explain his commitment to the Lord.

The young lady was not overjoyed. "Where is your head at, Ken? You're not the guy I used to know."

"That's right. I've met the Lord and He's really getting into my life."

"Okay, then I'm getting out," she fired back. "I don't want to go with some nutty Jesus Freak."

"Hey, wait a minute! I'm no freak. I don't plan to go around doing crazy way out things. I'm just into it with the Lord and I want to share that with people. It's only done good things in my life. What's wrong with that?"

Apparently in her mind there was plenty wrong with that. Even before the meal was over and she saw she could not get Ken back to his old ways, she got up and walked out.

She left Ken with the bill. He paid it and drove home.

Many of his buddies had similar reactions. To them smartening up to improve your life is equated with going soft. But not to all the group. Pete, for one, respected Ken's position and came to our office to talk about his own life and needs. We were to make a real friend of this young man.

The one Ken wanted to share with most of all was his tightest partner, Frank.

Frank couldn't understand why Ken even stayed around to wait for court. "If I had a beef like yours going, I'd split the country," he repeatedly told Ken. But as long as Ken wouldn't even consider such a possibility, Frank had an alternative ready.

"Let's you and me team up. With the charges on you and our reps, we don't need no gang. Nobody will stand up to us now. And what more can they do to you than what you're charged with? We can really let this town know we're around."

"No, Frank, that's not my trip anymore."

Ken thought Frank would laugh, but his old partner didn't. Actually he seemed almost happy for his friend. He listened while Kenny explained and then commented, "If that's what you did, Kenny, I don't want to put you down for it. I guess this is where you go your way and I go mine."

"Yes, I guess so," Ken replied, feeling keenly the separation he felt was at hand. "But we've been buddies a long time, and I'd sure like to see us together rather than me up in heaven and you down in hell."

"Hey, Ken, get off it," Frank responded. "That Jesus stuffy, it's just not for me. I'm sorry but that's the way it is."

The two boys shook hands, said good-bye and parted. They have had little contact since. Frank has been arrested on several serious felony counts and is awaiting court action. Many of the crowd feel he is trying to outdo Ken on getting in major trouble. Ken can do nothing now but pray for his former partner.

Ken was at court to say good-bye to Sam when he was sentenced. Sam was glad the wait was over, He could serve his time and then come out and build a good life for his future. He assured us that that was what he planned to do.

Actually Sam was very fortunate going to the California Youth Authority instead of to prison. He was later assigned to a college education program at Karl Holton School in Stockton.

But Sam's sentencing must surely have affected Ken. He couldn't help but know that the same day of judgment would soon come for him with no guarantee the result would be so favorable. But for the moment he had a while longer to wait and things to do.

CHAPTER 7

"Wonderful to Know You're Loved"

"I'm in a real jam. They're going to put me back in jail!" was the startling news Ken had for me on the phone. He sounded serious but I had to make sure. There were times when he called with news like that, and it was only his idea of a good joke.

But this was no joke. A detective had showed up at his dad's construction plant with an arrest warrant for Ken.

"Stay calm, Ken," I urged him. "Tell me what this is all about. What is the charge?"

"Attempted extortion, man. Remember that deal with Bill at the restaurant a while back and the phone calls from him? The D.A. is saying I tried to rip the cat off for some coin and they're busting me!" Ken heatedly replied.

"Have they set bail on the charge?"

"Yeah, they sure have. And get this: It's $50,000! Oh, wow, wait till my dad picks up on that figure."

I told Ken I'd notify his attorneys and we'd be in touch with him shortly. "In the meantime don't hassle the officer, just go along calmly and we'll find out what is going on."

I called the attorneys and we arranged to meet at the detective bureau a few hours later to go over the evidence on this new charge. Frankly I was worried. I was just sure the authorities must have some strong, compelling evidence Ken had not told me about in order to file such a serious charge and request the high bail. Certainly I knew about the encounter with Bill at the restaurant, the phone calls, and Ken's interviews with the detectives. But now I was wondering if Ken had been totally honest with me, and that bothered me a great deal.

The lawyers and I met with the detective assigned to the case, the same officer who was in charge of the murder investigation and who, coincidentally, was the same officer handling Sam Free's case. He was a man I had come to respect greatly. Detective Sergeant David Pascual would be a credit to any law enforcement agency: thorough, considerate, frank, well trained, honest. He is the kind of officer who comes to mind, raising anger in the average citizen who hears a man carrying a badge called a "pig." He deserves so much better than that and so do most of his colleagues. That it was this officer who had prepared the case only added to my gloom.

The detective told us about the initial contact between Ken and Bill at the restaurant and what had been said. There was nothing new there. Ken had told me about that. Next, we heard the tapes of the phone calls from Bill to Ken, calls we now learned had been made under the supervision of the police and recorded. I took careful notes as the recordings were played.

When the detective finished his presentation, I wanted to ask, "What else do you have?" But I remained silent, waiting for the reaction from Ken's attorneys.

"Is there any more evidence?" asked Mr. Pestarino.

"That's basically it," replied the detective.

The three of us were amazed—the attorneys, because a case had been built on what to them appeared such flimsy evidence; and I, because I heard nothing Ken had not previously told me. In fact, Ken's reaccounting of the events to me had been remarkably complete and accurate.

His attorneys and I had no doubt that Ken had been unwise to become involved in a feud between two young men, even trying to keep one from being hurt by urging payment to the other. But repeatedly on the police tapes, Ken said he wanted nothing for himself and was only trying to help Bill. Unwise for Ken in his position? Yes. But a crime? Not in his attorneys' view.

Mr. Pestarino was angry and outside the sheriff's office he gave his associate and me his reasons.

"That is a terribly weak case and the district attorney must know it. He must be trying to get Ken off the streets and make things harder on the murder case. And we're going to have to let him know we won't go along on this," he firmly stated.

"You may believe it's not a valid case, but the press and television won't see it that way," I added. "This story will get a big play with a murder suspect picked up on a new charge."

And indeed it did.

Mr. Roessler and I went to meet with an impatient Mr. Pestana, anxious for a report on his son. He was not a happy man.

"Look, I put up 200 grand to get that kid of mine out on a murder charge, and now he turns around and gets picked up for extortion. What is it going to take to teach him?" Mr. Pestana asked in blunt, direct terms. "I told him to stay away from those hoods who get into trouble and then this happens. Well, I'm not getting him out again. If he's that stupid, he can just stay in jail. That just might be where he belongs!"

Even when we told Ken's father that keeping his son locked up was probably what the prosecution wanted, and refusing to have the youth released now was almost an admission of guilt to the community, he would not budge.

"I've had it with that kid, do you hear me?" he responded. "Them coming into my plant and hauling my son off in handcuffs in front of all my workers. How much more do I have to put up with from him?" Answering his own question he concluded, "I'm through."

The man was not about to budge. I called Mr. Pestarino to pass the message on to Ken that he was going to be locked up for a while. I was too upset to go and tell him myself at that time; besides, I wanted to find out what I could about the threats against Bill, the basis for the charge.

That was not hard to do. That same evening Ken's buddy Pete filled me in on the ill-feeling between Bill and a number of the group, especially Frank. Pete gave me a written statement which I passed on to both the detective and Ken's attorneys.

Naturally our counseling ministry to Ken stopped while he was in lock-up. When we did talk together at the jail he was nervous, concerned, and fully aware of the impact the new charge would have on his major case.

"I always liked the sergeant. I guess I still do but he really messed me over on this one," Ken commented. "The only thing they've got here is something to hurt me in the community and in court. But the prosecutor can sure use this to further convince himself I'm really a bad dude."

Ken's conclusion was right. But he did manage to keep in fairly good spirits. He had a copy of *The Way* in his cell and caught up a good deal on his reading.

The preliminary hearing was set for two weeks after Ken's arrest, and during most of that period Ken's father remained adament in his refusal to help Ken. Mr. Pestana did visit his son one day after a tiring, frustrating business trip and took out his feelings in a strong tirade on Ken. Later Mr. Pestana told me he felt badly about the interview, and I assured him Ken would appreciate knowing that.

A few days before the hearing, Mr. Pestana saw a press story detailing how Ken's wealthy father had posted $200,000 to get his son out on bail for murder but so far had not secured the boy's release when the bail was an additional $50,000. That did it. What the attorneys and I couldn't get Mr. Pestana to do, the press accomplished for us. "What do they mean?" he angrily asked as we talked in his office at the house. "They think it's a matter of money, so now I won't help my son. They're crazy. He's been in long enough on this." Mr. Pestana called his attorney and said he wanted Ken released no matter how much had to be posted.

"The hearing is only two days away; let's wait until then," counseled Mr. Roessler, completely reversing the positions the two men had taken since Ken was arrested.

"All right," replied Mr. Pestana, "but mark my word, Thursday he gets out."

And Mr. Pestana is a man of his word. He came to court and brought the family to show support for Ken, which greatly encouraged and surprised the boy. He also had the necessary papers to instantly post any amount of bail the court might order.

In a preliminary hearing, a felony case is brought before a magistrate to show that a crime has been committed and the possibility that the defendant committed it. That is all that is necessary to have a case bound over for trial in Superior Court where the requirements for conviction are much stronger: guilt beyond a reasonable doubt and to a moral certainty. Thus at the preliminary hearing, the prosecution usually gets a case transferred without much problem, and the defense presents no evidence, preferring to wait for the trial itself to answer the charges. However, at Ken's hearing the defense did respond.

The prosecutor opened by calling to the stand a youth who had been with Bill in the restaurant the night Bill and Ken met. He had heard part of the conversation. Two tapes of Bill's calls to Ken were then played. Ken kept fairly calm while this was going on, occasionally whispering a clarifying correction of fact to me, sitting with him at the table with the defense counsel. On the witness stand he answered the questions from both sides in a polite, careful and straightforward manner. One thing we knew when he was through: he would do well for himself whenever he testified.

I took the stand to confirm briefly that Ken had told me the details of the events in the case prior to his arrest as they happened, an action that would have been highly unlikely if he indeed were committing a crime.

The judge ruled that the minimal requirements for ordering a trial had been met, but he sounded an ominous note for the prosecution, commenting that there were substantial issues in the case a jury might well debate before reaching a verdict. Ken took the judge's remarks to mean the jurist did not consider the case a strong one.

As for a trial being ordered, we expected it. The really important question of the day was Ken's bail—still set at $50,000 on this charge and $200,000 bond on the murder charge.

The prosecutor wanted the $50,000 bail figure left as it was—in fact, from his remarks at the end, Ken almost expected Mr. Davies to ask that the figure be raised. The defense wanted Ken released on his own recognizance without bail. That wasn't quite what was done but Ken came close. The judge set bail at $1,000 and ruled that the current bond for release was adequate to cover the new one. As soon as the papers were processed Ken would get out.

I took care of that matter for the family, but it wasn't as simple as it might appear. The chief problem was with jail officials. The officers never believed Ken would gain his release on the murder charge, and now they found it all but impossible to comprehend how the youth could get out on still another charge. But they finally convinced themselves that the release papers were indeed valid, and Ken was on his way home.

Mr. Russell Roessler, one of Ken's attorneys, reviews pending court actions with the defendent.

Those next few weeks were busy ones for Ken. He worked at his father's yard even though many of his friends derided him for working at a time when he knew he was going to be locked up for a long time.

"You can make more money in an hour ripping off places than you can in that yard in a month," one of his old partners argued. "Besides, it would be a lot less strain." Ken patiently explained he was out of the ripping-off business, and working to pay back his dad for some of the help Ken had received was just fine with him.

He took over production of my weekly radio phone-in talk show for students, "Speak Out," heard Sunday nights on KLIV. In that capacity he not only screened all the callers before they came on the air but met many of the community leaders who were my guests. Ken liked the assignment. During the interviews he found a number of people who were quite startled when they recognized his name from all the publicity he had had. He did an outstanding job. He also recorded a radio special on his experiences for the Christian stations of the Family Radio Network out of San Fransisco.

Ken made many new friends, especially when he spent a week at the Campus Life training session for our volunteer college staff at Palm Springs. He enjoyed meeting and dating a number of Christian girls, friendships I very much encouraged. Interestingly enough, Ken had few problems with the parents of his new friends. They seemed to like and accept him readily despite his notoriety, though the parental approval was not unanimous.

When the major league baseball teams come to play either the San Fransisco Giants or the Oakland A's, I often conduct the chapel program for them. Ken joined me when I met with the Philadelphia Phillies, the Montreal Expos, and the Cincinnati Reds. With each team he shared quietly and carefully what the Lord had come to mean in his life, and derived much encouragement from meeting many outstanding ball players firmly committed in their own faith. Ken took his brother, John, along to the meetings as well.

During this time, he also returned to the James Boys Ranch—not as a ward of the court, but to share with the young fellows his experiences and what he had learned. There was rapt attention in the rec hall as 80 fellows, all Ken's age or only a year or so younger, listened as this young man about whom they had all heard so much spoke: "I'd give anything if I were coming back to this ranch instead of what I face. I hope you guys appreciate what you've got here. A lot of good things can come down if you'll get with it.

"When I first got here I blew it—and pretty bad. And I was wrong. I made a lot of crazy moves, and Mr. Martin over there probably still has the scars to prove it.

"But he's my friend now and I really like the guy.

"After I got my thinking straightened out, I did all right. I picked up a few sports awards, picked up on school and counseling and made it out in record time.

"I didn't make it on the outside. What I want you guys here to know is that the ranch is not to blame for my failure. I am. These people gave it a good try. I'm the one who didn't. They can do only so much, and if a guy is making it in the program, then sooner or later he has to be released. After that it's up to him.

"I wish I had stayed in school instead of just causing trouble. I also wish my parents and I had gotten along, but we didn't. Then, too, I should have had enough smarts to know that a bad crowd can ruin you, no matter how smart or wise you think you are. That's true even

While awaiting trial, Ken joins with Gordon McLean to share in a Campus Life meeting at the James Boys Ranch.

though I did most of the leading. That street scene was a real bummer.

"It's bad enough that I got things loused up for me and my family, but a lot of innocent people got hurt as well. I put a lot of scars on faces and even more in hearts. One night I drove a guy I knew from the ranch to a store, and he went in and blew a young clerk away. I get sick whenever I think of it.

"If all this sounds bad, well, it is. But, there are a few good things on the good side though.

"I'm in tight with the Lord now. He and I are close partners. Don't ask me if that's really true. If it wasn't I sure wouldn't be here talking with you guys tonight. They wouldn't want me on the ranch, and I would have long since split the scene to stay out of jail as long as possible. Someday they would have caught me, but a lot of things would have gone down first.

"But I'm gonna stick it out even though some of the old partners tell me I'm crazy.

"Those guys don't know where I'm at. They never read a Bible, say a prayer, or know what it means to ask the Lord to guide you and have Him do it. They're missing something. Maybe I'm not the unlucky one after all.

"Sure, I got this big beef I'm up against, and it gets to me at times. I'm not getting out of it, but I know God is gonna be with me no matter how much time I get. My old partners haven't got the big beefs yet, though some of them will if they keep up what they're doin'. But they ain't got the Lord either and without Him it's nowhere.

"If I had the choice of getting a short sentence without the Lord or taking the big beef in the joint knowing God was with me, I'd stick it out with Him, no matter how long. There is no way I'm going back to what I was. I hope you guys feel the same way."

When he finished Ken was surrounded by numbers of the guys asking questions and wishing him well. He talked with the wards for the rest of the evening and also received the best wishes and offers of help from a number of the staff, including several counselors with whom Ken had his most serious run-ins. It was a good night.

Not everyone appreciated having in their midst a young man out on bail for murder. Nor was it always easy for Ken. He had to get used to being stopped regularly by patrolmen as he drove his car. He was constantly questioned, searched and checked for outstanding traffic tickets and warrants.

One unnerving incident took place one hot evening as we were returning late from a meeting. Ken decided to stop at a Seven/Eleven store for an icy soft drink. The store was deserted except for us and the high-school-age clerk behind the counter.

The boy told us he worked the night shift alone and Ken asked casually, "Don't you think it might be dangerous?"

The clerk replied that this store had never been robbed, though others nearby had been hit. "In fact," he added, "at one of our stores a while back a clerk was shot and killed."

Startled, I looked at Ken. He was very somber and asked quietly, "What happened?"

"This young man named Al came in, robbed the store, got the money, and then fired a shot at the clerk. There were two or three of them. Some guy named Ken drove the truck they used for a getaway. They were a couple of real bad hoods. Man, that was a terrible scene!"

I was now thoroughly alarmed at the turn in the conversation. If this young clerk were to find out who was standing in front of him, he might panic. The worse thing that could happen now would be for Ken to identify himself.

And then it happened.

"Let me shake hands with you," Ken said in a friendly manner. "My name is Ken Pestana, and I'm the fellow you're talking about. But I may not be quite the hood you described. Think about that and good luck to you."

That did it.

"Ken," I said firmly, "we're leaving right now. Come on."

Ken walked out quietly and got into my car. He knew I was angry but couldn't understand why.

"I'll tell you why!" I heatedly responded. "You scared that young man half to death! He turned white as a ghost; he probably thinks I'm your accomplice."

Ken laughed at that. "I'd never consider you for the job. You can't run fast enough."

"Cut the funny stuff," I continued. "I'm taking you right to your house and when I come back here on my way home, I'll guarantee that this place will be crawling with police. Don't ever do that again!"

I had to press my point strongly. Ken had

done nothing wrong, but if by some quirk of fate that store had been robbed that night or even in the few weeks following, there would have been no way that Ken could have avoided being a suspect. Fortunately nothing happened, but the police were indeed there when I passed by a short time later.

A few days later Ken applied to work as a clerk at a small convenience store. He used his right name but had to reject the position because of his 9 p.m. court-ordered curfew. He explained he wanted to know the problems and dangers in a store from a clerk's point of view. It might have been an interesting education.

Perhaps the most important things happening to Ken were with his family. After his second release we sat in the family kitchen until 2 in the morning talking with his mother and dad.

"Ken," his dad said, "I really want to know what is going on with you. This has been hard on all of us. That's why I blew up at you in jail last Saturday and I'm sorry I did."

The young man looked up startled, and responded, "Dad, that's the first time you ever told me you were sorry and that you had been wrong."

"Well, I meant it. Often I've been too busy to be close to you and the other children. This business just keeps me going day and night. Here it is 11:30 at night and I'm just getting home for dinner. No wonder we've been strangers."

"Dad, I always wanted to please you and Mom," Ken responded, feeling the tension between him and his parents. "I couldn't do it or just didn't know how or something. I just felt you were down on me. What I did wasn't good enough. So pretty soon I quit trying. Then I didn't care what I did."

"But Kenny," his mother interjected, "didn't you know how much you were hurting us when you went out and did all those wrong things?"

There was a long pause as Ken looked down at the floor, weighing his response carefully, and then looked back at his parents. The moment of truth had come.

"Why do you think I did them? At least when I was bad I was noticed, someone paid attention to me; for at least a little while I mattered."

Despite the strong thoughts and deep emotion in the room, there were no loud voices raised, no intemperate outbursts; rather, it was a family talking seriously—perhaps for the first time in the years letting out long held resentments and bitterness.

"Maybe I deserve that statement, son, but your mother certainly doesn't," Mr. Pestana quietly countered. "She's spent hours with all of you children. When you had a paper route, she often got up on rainy, cold mornings and drove the car to help you deliver papers. She even paid your bill when you got behind. She wanted all of you to have the things that were right and good."

"But what I needed most was not just help. I needed to know I belonged here. I wanted someone to care for me, not if I did certain things right or got good grades or made it in sports. I wanted to be loved just for what I am, a person, a son. That was missing. It really was," Ken stated.

"Ken, what is it you asked God to do in your life a few weeks back?" I interposed.

"Come into my life, change me, and forgive me for doing so much wrong," Ken answered.

"You asked God to forgive you, right?" I continued.

Ken nodded, "Yes."

"But how can you ask God to forgive you for what you've done until you are ready to forgive those you think have hurt you? Remember the section of the Lord's Prayer, 'Forgive us our trespasses as we forgive those who trespass against us'? You have to forgive your parents and anybody else you may feel has wronged you before you can come to God and ask Him to accept you."

"Your father and I made our mistakes, Ken," his mother added, "but maybe you weren't willing to accept love when it was there. Love has to be received, and it comes in many different forms."

The discussion was lengthy but the time passed quickly. It was like lancing a sore to let out a festering infection, a necessary step to healing. But the healing was there, and I believe God was at work that night in the hearts of some very broken people. That kind of emotional healing takes time.

It was Ken's mother who had the last word. "We've all learned a lot tonight. It's too bad it had to come this way. But, Kenny, we love you very much. We want what is best for you, and we're going to help you all we can. Count on that."

Ken walked out to my car and wanted to talk some more, so we sat on the driveway and Ken poured out his heart.

"I know they love me. They showed it when they posted $200,000 to get me out and then when they all came to court, ready to post everything they had if I needed it to get out on this second charge.

"And I love them. I'm through hurting them. They ought to have a better life than I've given them."

I didn't interrupt him. He kept talking, tears filling his eyes.

"Why did it have to take this mess in my life for it to happen, for my folks and I to get it together, to start talking, loving, and really caring for each other? So many people got hurt, a kid got blown away, I'm goin' to the joint for a lot of years, then it happens—we really get on with each other.

"Gordy, if it takes me goin' away for a long time, then I still think it was worth it. A lot of guys in jail think nobody cares, and they're right. I've got it so much better. I know God loves me, I know you're my friend, and I know my people are behind me no matter what."

He stopped to brush the tears out of his eyes with his sleeve.

"Hey, man, I don't cry easy. I've been beat up a few times, hurt and worked over and it don't matter. It's been years since I felt like this. It's wonderful to know you're loved."

Ken was choked up, struggling for words, trying to find a way of expressing the well of emotion built up inside.

"I don't have to be the tough guy anymore, the young gangster. I don't have to prove I'm all big and bad. I can just be me . . . with my family . . . my girl friend . . . and with the Lord."

I reached for his hand and let him keep talking.

"I don't know how to say it, man. I just don't know. It's so good now, but why . . . why . . . why did it have to come this way?"

Neither of us spoke for a few minutes. Finally I broke the silence of the night. "I can't answer your question. I don't know if anybody can. Ken, just know that when you're loved, it's the greatest thing in the world."

CHAPTER 8

"Somebody Up There Likes You"

Mike lives in the Mexican section of Azusa, an area suffering from neglect and lack of opportunity for its young people. That he's been in trouble is not too surprising; it would be amazing to reach age fifteen in his neighborhood and not be arrested. Burglary and car theft were the formal charges on his juvenile court petition, but they represent only a part of his law violations.

Mike is a husky, darkly handsome youth with strong leadership qualities, and it was this potential that caused the probation officer to recommend Mike for the Lifeline camp sponsored by the Youth Guidance department of Campus Life in Covina. The invitation was extended by director Sonny Trujillo, and Mike was off to camp at Silver Valley Ranch.

The camp was a pleasant change for the boy a few days before school started. There were fifty other fellows and girls like Mike there, all of them referred by police or probation agencies. Ken Pestana was there, too, as a counselor and guest speaker.

"You should see these kids," Ken told me on the phone. "There are kids eight, nine and ten with switchblades. One kid had booze in his canteen—he was eight; and another nine-year-old offered me a hit off a joint he smuggled in. I can't believe it!"

As for Mike, he wasn't too interested in people talking about God. But despite his indifferent front, the boy really wanted to change, quit drugs, and make something useful out of his life and future. Those were desires he would never share with an adult, but he did relate them to Ken on the second day of camp, and the two became good friends.

When Ken spoke to the group and told them of his own experiences and current troubles with the law and the courts, Mike really listened. First, Ken was in more trouble than Mike could begin to imagine; and second, Ken had found a personal faith that gave him both a quiet confidence and the power to change the wrong things in his life. That's what appealed to Mike.

And he responded. As converted ex-convict Phil Thatcher gave the invitation to accept Christ after Ken spoke, Mike was the second boy to step forward for prayer. He meant it no matter how his peers reacted. As it turned out, many of them made the same spiritual commitment and Ken, a young Christian himself, had his hands full helping other young new believers grow in their faith. He also collected an assortment of zip guns, switchblades, and lids of grass many of his young hearers removed when they put New Testaments in their packs.

It was a responsibility Ken enjoyed, especially when Mike came across the state a few weeks later to be Ken's guest at his home.

With Jack it was different. He was older, no stranger to trouble or to Ken. Ever since they both were six years of age, Ken and Jack had been tied together by the tangled web of frustration, rebellion, and delinquency.

With Jack it was rip-offs and drugs, using and dealing, that landed him in a state youth institution. Jack had problems all right, but from what he heard, what his friend Ken faced was far worse.

Soon after his release Jack looked up Ken and learned the full story of all that had occurred. Jack had been close to the tragic events of that December night—in fact, for a short time he himself was a suspect in the case and had a subpoena, issued at the request of the district attorney, to testify at the trial.

So Jack expected to learn details about a robbery and murder, but he didn't expect to see Ken clean, thinking straight, and very much enthusiastic over his experience with the Lord.

"Let me tell you, I know Kenny," Jack commented, "and we don't play any con games on each other. This God thing he was into was no cop out, no snow job for the courts. He really meant it. He's still human and he's got problems, but my old buddy sure isn't the guy he used to be."

"Talk on, brother," Jack responded when Ken shared with his friend what the Lord could do in a guy's life. Pete, Ken's friend from the boys' ranch, had the same reaction, becoming increasingly interested in what had happened spiritually to his buddy.

Both Jack and Pete were on hand to help

with a unique project: helping Ken put the events described in this book into a special Family Films movie production released across the nation. The picture was filmed in the area where the real events happened and features Ken, his family, law enforcement officials, and many of his old pals, including Jack and Pete.

The long hours of filming and the emotional strain of recreating events he would like to forget were hard on Ken, but he never waivered in giving the cameras his very best effort. The result is a moving, factual, challenging color film production that speaks to the hearts of both young people and their parents.

In addition to making the film, the weeks awaiting trial gave me an opportunity to sample community feeling about Ken and his friends. A lawyer is often identified with his cases and receives criticism for representing unpopular clients. The same is true of a minister. Since I was known as a friend of a young man facing a murder charge, I received some similar negative response.

School teachers were divided between those who were happy to be rid of the troublemakers and those who felt the guys in Ken's group could be helped. Certainly none of the crowd have been good students. One teacher told me, "The only culture that group has been exposed to is bacteria."

Parents in the neighborhood reacted against Ken and even his younger brother, John. Several of John's friends were no longer permitted to come to the Pestana home after Ken was released on bail. That action hurt John deeply, but it also helped bring the two brothers even closer together.

As might be expected, most of the patrolmen in the area familiar with Ken and company were not among the fellows' admirers. "They've got a lot of character all right," one told me, "and all of it bad."

"Did any of the group work?" I asked an official.

"The only guy I know who worked steadily was a spray painter for a hot-car garage!" he replied.

One older gentleman described Ken and his pals in these precise, bitter terms: "Those boys would lift a blind man's wallet, feed poisoned Alpo to his seeing-eye dog, help the man safely halfway across the freeway, and then say 'Good luck, mister' as they left him there."

As for the young people in the area, they somewhat admired the group for their daring but were careful to keep their distance. "They were always ready to lend a helping fist," one youth wryly commented.

Ken was fully aware of the bad feelings about him, even understood them, but it is still not surprising that he had periods of depression. What was amazing was his ability to recover from them so quickly. Even the strongest person would have a great emotional reaction to his own murder trial and the thought of long years of confinement, plus knowing many people in the community were down on him. He felt all those things keenly.

Ken's low points only showed how genuinely human he is and his recovery demonstrated the strength the Lord can give in the midst of real adversity. And there was no doubt that Ken's strength did indeed come from Christ. Few mature adults could handle what Ken faced. He, as a teen-ager, did more than well in coping with a critical situation, even though he brought it on himself.

Ken had courage; without it he never would have been in the trouble he was. However, it's important to remember that courage and convictions are not the same thing. Many young people are given credit for having strong, honest standards when really they are merely cowards. It's not that they don't want to do wrong or fear being caught; they are simply afraid of doing the act, and so they back down. Ken had no such reluctance; he did many brazenly wrong things. Only when he met the Lord did he add convictions and values to his courage. And his was certainly an interesting change in life-style, and the difference was readily noticeable.

"There were many days when I wanted to split the whole scene," Ken explains. "One of my partners out on bail on another charge stole a car and bogeyed. He came by and asked me to go with him, and it was sure tempting. And believe me there were days when a one-way ticket to Nairobi was not only interesting, it was downright inviting.

"I lived through the tragic nightmare of the case night after night for six months on murder max row. Even when I got out and tasted freedom, the events of the past and the future were never far from my mind. Every day brought me closer to reliving the whole tragedy again—this time in a courtroom before the gaze of a judge, a jury, the press, and the whole community.

"I told God how I hated to go through it. He said He'd be there with me. One day I found a verse in the Bible that just blew my mind: 'When you are arrested, don't worry about what to say at your trial, for you will be given the right words at the right time. For it won't be you doing the talking—it will be the Spirit of your Heavenly Father speaking through you!' (Matt. 10:19, 20).

"When I complained about how rough it was, God reminded me that His Son went through worse for me. When I worried about being lonely and cut off from my people, He said Jesus had been through that trip and He would bring me out all right in the end. I never question that I deserved what was happening.

"I believed the Lord could bring me out, but it's hard to accept that when everyone and everything is coming down on you. However, it was a choice of trusting God for His strength, or splitting and being hunted down, or blowing my mind and breaking under the pressure. I chose the first route.

"I'd kick back and dig into *The Way* to see what God had to say. Then I'd talk to Him—no big words or church lingo, just how I felt. When I was upset or blowing it, I told Him, and I was always stronger after I had talked it out with Him. I even got so I could talk to God about the needs of other people, including some of my older partners. It was neat."

Not all the responses to Ken were negative, however. Many Christian people and groups in the community were kind and did accept him. He was well received when he visited several youth groups, and one church, which he never visited, sent him a gracious letter from the congregation assuring him of their prayers and concern for his future. He was deeply touched by it.

Another encouragement was a letter to the court from Earlie Thomas of the New York *Jets* football team. "Our team very much appreciated meeting and hearing Ken speak at one of our chapel programs. We all were greatly impressed by his sincerity, and believe God has His hand on this young man."

A girl at a church youth group told me, "Ken helped me really see how God works in peoples' lives in a practical, real way. He's sure down-to-earth about his faith and how he feels about his problems."

After months of waiting, most of the delays caused by Al's appeals, Ken and Al finally came to trial in Superior Court. Our film had been finished late the night before, and Ken was still tired as he sat beside Mr. Pestarino for the opening of court.

At the back of the room sat the mother of the young man slain in the robbery. She looked very uncomfortable in the presence of the accused slayers of her son, and yet she wanted to be there. A few rows away sat Ken's mother equally unhappy at the circumstances that brought her to the courtroom.

Here indeed was an ironic situation: one

mother had lost a son to a cruel killer; another, could well lose her boy to prison. The two women had something deeply in common, but it was a grief they could not share with each other.

Ken noticed the mother of the victim and felt a deep sorrow over having even a part in her tragedy. Courtroom ethics would not permit him to talk with her. Perhaps that was best, since any expression would have been difficult for Ken, and the mother of the deceased youth might not have wanted to hear anything he would say. So when the two passed in the courtroom halls, each looked away.

As court began, the first item of business was a motion by the prosecutor to cancel Ken's bail and remand him to custody. The deputy district attorney argued that at this point bail was not a right but entirely discretionary with the judge. He was right. Further, he argued that several tapes made at the time of Ken's arrest for murder showed him to be a dangerous person, and his later arrest for extortion while on bail only reenforced that belief.

The judge decided that only the tapes on the extortion matter were relevant to the issue of bail, so the murder trial began with what amounted to a hearing on an extortion charge. It was practically a repeat of the preliminary hearing with the tapes of the alleged offense being played and my taking the stand to again assert that Ken had told me of the events as they happened in that case, hardly realistic conduct if an extortion atttempt were indeed being made.

After careful consideration the judge denied

the prosecution motion, and Ken would be free for the trial. Jury selection was to begin first thing the next morning.

Too many people think arrest implies guilt, and a trial merely a game to see which side has the sharpest lawyer. That a person is innocent until proven guilty beyond a reasonable doubt and to a moral certainty is a sound principle of law; indeed it is at the very heart of our trial system, but it is also highly suspect if not totally rejected by large numbers of our citizens. To these people guilt or innocence are lost to the overriding belief that if a person is accused of a crime, he must be guilty, and a slick lawyer is trying to find some gimmick or legal loophole to turn a criminal loose on an already anxious society. For that reason few criminal lawyers win popularity contests.

A juror's lot may not be a happy one either. The job of decision maker can be a difficult challenge for the average citizen who sits, perhaps unwillingly, on a jury. No matter how incomplete the evidence, let that juror vote for anything less than full guilt in a notorious case and he will have more than a little answering to do when he confronts his disgusted neighbors, co-workers, and perhaps his own family. Of course in other situations it would be a guilty verdict that would bring down peer group wrath.

In this case several prospective jurors expressed belief in the guilt of the accused before hearing any evidence, and they were promptly excused by the judge along with others who pleaded legitimate hardship in serving for what could be a lengthy trial.

One juror tried to hide his prejudice and appear impartial, but careful questioning by the attorneys finally showed him to be anything but open-minded. He was dropped from the panel.

A juror who was acceptable to both sides startled the court by saying he had been in contact with the law at a very early age.

"In juvenile hall?" the judge asked.

"Not exactly," the man replied. "My father and my mother were both sheriffs in another state."

The courtroom rang with laughter.

"My father was elected, then died before completing his term of office, so my mother served in his place," the man explained.

A college student juror was excused when she told the court she overidentified with people and their problems and could not be objective.

When court adjourned for the day, ten prospective jurors were seated.

The next morning jury selection stopped as the judge, attorneys, and the defendants were in earnest negotiations in an attempt to end the case without trial.

Such dickering, called plea-bargaining, is often frowned on in the community when it allows a defendant to plead guilty to a lesser charge than the original and receive a more modest sentence. But in turn for that plea the state is spared the time and expense of a trial and so is sharing some of the advantages of that saving with the accused. Frankly, if it were not for such accepted pleas, our already overcrowded criminal court dockets would be an absolute nightmare with trials not called for many years. Despite the critics, plea-bargaining is generally sound practice.

Actually for Al there was little offered. He would have to plead guilty to first degree murder and go to prison, but he would be spared the agony of a trial in which there was no doubt what the result would be. The prosecution had a perfect case to present, and no one knew it better than Bill Cottrell, the very talented, dedicated public defender who gave generously of his time to be both counsel and friend to his young client.

For Ken, who had not handled a weapon or pulled a trigger, there would be a guilty plea with the judge determining the degree of the offense and also the sentence, with either prison or the Youth Authority the most likely choices. His attorneys would be able to present views on Ken's sentencing at a hearing.

That was not only a reasonable settlement but exactly what Ken's attorneys had been striving to arrange for six months. However, both boys would have to plead for the arrangement to be complete, and there was no guarantee that Al would agree.

Al talked at length with both his attorney and Ken and told them he would do anything to help Ken. That was not enough for Al's attorney who made it clear to Al that admitting guilt was the right thing to do for himself. Al asked to consider his decision overnight and that request was granted.

The next morning Al told the court he would plead guilty, acknowledging that it was he who had shot and killed the young clerk in the store. It was a hard decision for the young man, and there was suddenly a general feeling of sympathy for him in the closed courtroom. While many believed Al deserved life imprisonment for his callous crime, few gained any real satisfaction watching him accept that heavy judgment.

Then Ken, too, pleaded guilty to murder, admitting his voluntary participation in the armed robbery that had resulted in death. The prosecutor, usually unyielding to a defendant on the stand, was gentle and almost kind to the young men in questioning them as to their pleas. Surprisingly he did not ask that Ken be placed in custody pending sentence, a motion that most likely would have been granted at that point.

Now there would be no trial, but a very important question remained to be answered: would Ken go to prison?

Should he?

"Why of course," many would say, "if only as a deterrent to others who may go out and commit crime."

But is punishment a deterrent? Admittedly, there are firmly committed experts on both sides of that question. I feel strongly on the matter. No young person I know who committed a crime ever gave a moment of thought to the possible punishment for the simple reason he never expected to be caught. And frankly on that issue the odds are with the criminal. Further, it may be wise to ask if punishing one person to deter another is even morally right.

In a recent year, 723,936 cases of seven major felonies were reported in California. Of that number, felony complaints issued in only 14.6 percent of the cases; 3.6 percent of the total were not convicted; 9.8 percent received probation, jail or a fine; and 1.4 percent of the total crimes reported resulted in an offender going to a state institution, a figure that hardly speaks well for imprisonment as a deterrent to crime. The potential criminal may be more impressed with his 85.2 percent chance of not even being apprehended or the 98.6 percent chance he will avoid long confinement if he is arrested.

"Actually the main reason prisons are filled is the cry of society for punishment and revenge," a prison official told me. "We find that concept hard to accept, so society masks its real intent around a much nicer sounding word—rehabilitation. In the name of rehabilitation we support a whole establishment of counselors, parole officers and the like who are much too intelligent to believe their work is related to anything more than warehousing offenders. The exchange is a good one: the correctional establishment makes a fine living and the citizens are allowed to maintain their kindly myth of rehabilitation behind walls."

How will Ken or any other young person come out of a prison experience? There are as many different answers to that question as there are individuals, but an understanding of the penal system in America will give us some clues as to what may happen.

Our correction official explains: "We send

people to college to train them to be teachers, doctors and lawyers. People going to prison are trained to be criminals, and the results are just as sure as they are for those in college. Not every graduate of medical school is a practicing physician, but most are. Not every ex-con is a criminal; some flunk the prison course and become good citizens. Perhaps they encountered a concerned chaplain, counselor, teacher, or foreman in the prison who helped them go against the tide, or maybe they gritted their teeth and decided to make the best of it. Upon release, they may also have gotten some good help from groups specializing in helping former prisoners. Or they may have found an employer brave enough to risk hiring an ex-con and giving that person a second chance. But those good results are not the general story.

"Why don't prisons work? Let me illustrate. Take a dog, put him in a cage for five years, kick him around, let him have limited exercise only, surround him with other fierce dogs. Then at the end of the time let the dog out. Are you surprised that he bites? What else could be expected? And that is what happens in prisons. When people come out they so often fight back."

Certainly there are those so depraved in our society that they need to be confined to protect the rest of us. Experienced prison officials put that number at about 15 percent of their inmate population.

"If we confine that 15 percent and concentrate our efforts on community programs and supervision for the rest, along with small, short-term facilities offering educational and training programs to groups of inmates placed together on the basis of age and maturity, we would be much further ahead," a prison warden told me.

"Human lives could be salvaged, tax dollars saved. Most important, there might well be fewer next victims to be hurt by the embittered graduates of our present crime schools."

Would Ken go to prison?

Neither his friends nor his enemies would decide that. Society, speaking through a judge, would make that choice.

Certainly imprisoning Ken was not apt to deter others; even the statistics indicate that. Much more important, it would not help the victim of the crime in which Ken had a part. And that was a major consideration. If locking up Ken for the rest of his life in the worst hell-hole that could be devised would restore the life of the young clerk, or genuinely ease the grief of that man's loved ones, then prison would seem like a small price to pay. But no punishment now given Ken or the young man who fired the fatal shots could alter the events or erase the memory of that horrible winter night. With real tragedy, consolation must come from God, not courtroom judgments.

"Prison may only undo all the good Ken has accomplished while he has been out on bail," Mr. Pestarino firmly stated as his reason for not imposing prison for his client. "He needs to build on his faith and strengths. He could use more education and he plans to get it. He has broken away from a criminally inclined gang and now faces the prospect of being thrown behind bars with a worse crowd than the one he has struggled to leave, and this during some of the most important years of his life. It hardly makes sense."

If Ken went to prison, rehabilitation would not be the goal—only revenge, and nothing else. And if that is the best our society can achieve, then perhaps our failure is as sad as Ken's.

Leaving court after the pleas, I stopped to talk with an investigator for the sheriff's office. He had some strong feelings on the case.

"I'm glad it's over. I had the miserable task of telling the victim's brother about the young man's death. He had come by the store to see how his brother was doing on the fourth night at work. I had to tell him he no longer had a brother. So you can feel for your friend, Ken," he pointedly remarked, "but I'm still thinking about the young fellow who lost his brother.

"Do me a favor, Mr. McLean. The next time you want to help a kid in trouble, don't settle for such a loser."

"I'm not sure I picked a loser this time," I quietly replied, ending the conversation.

Ken talked with Mr. Pestarino after court. "I was sure the district attorney was going to insist that I be locked up after my plea. Why didn't he do it?"

"I don't know, Ken. I expected it too," his attorney replied. "Somebody up there must really like you. Things have surely been going well."

Then catching the spirit of the events, the lawyer counseled his young client, "Just keep the faith, Kenny."

Ken would certainly do that. He relaxed, shook his attorney's hand, and left the courthouse to await his sentencing date three weeks away.

CHAPTER 9

"Everybody Has a Master"

"However sad their fate, there is one young man who would gladly change places with the two defendants before the court today if he could, and that is the young man for whose death they are responsible," affirmed the district attorney before a crowded but hushed courtroom at the sentencing of Ken and Al.

"I agree with the recommendation of the probation officer. Both of these young men should go to prison," he continued.

For Ken the wait was over. Finally, here in the courts, he would learn his fate. He had grown increasingly nervous as sentencing day approached and often ate little, certainly a human reaction to a major crisis. But he never wanted to quit his Christian activities. He still desired to keep busy sharing his experiences with various groups up until his last day in court.

And Ken had worked diligently at building his own strength in the Lord. "I am sure I'm going to need it," he earnestly remarked, admitting he expected the worst to happen in court. "But you know, when I'm at my weakest that is when the Lord is strongest and closest to me. This is hard to go through, but it would be impossible without Him."

In reading *The Way* Ken not only noticed that some of the greatest writings in the Bible were from Paul in prison, but he also noted that three of the greatest men in the Bible were murderers—Moses, David, and Paul.

"I drove the truck and Paul held the coats while the crowd stoned Stephen. I guess we're about the same!" Ken earnestly pointed out.

Of course Ken had something else he shared with Paul—an experience with the Lord and a faith on which to build a new life even in a prison cell.

And Ken got encouragement in that direction from a young man who could relate to Ken's situation better than the most understanding on-looker, Art DePeralta, sitting in a federal prison cell for his part in a sensational local bank robbery-kidnapping case, a story I've told in the book *Hell Bent Kid*.

Art, who knew Ken only slightly, was tremendously concerned for his acquaintance facing prison. Art often phoned to check on the progress of the case, to encourage Ken, and to share some good advice for a young man facing confinement.

"Behind bars is no easy place to live a Christian life or build your faith, and to survive as a young guy, there are some rough choices you have to make in tight situations," Art wisely counseled out of his own firsthand experience. "But you can come out all right. You've really got to decide which side you're on and stick to it, no matter how much the pressure or how heavy the misunderstandings. There are a lot of guys, including religious ones, in the joint playing games, and you've got to watch out for the phonies.

"On the other hand, the evil people behind bars are at least very real. It is easier to be really evil than really good, and real evil always wins over phony goodness.

"Ken, you've got to submit to someone. The only question is to whom. Everybody has a master. Jesus gives us a choice: mastery by Him is freedom; mastery by anyone else, including ourselves, is slavery.

"Some cons will try to entice you, then manipulate, dominate, and finally destroy you. You have just got to be a little sharper, and as one of the younger guys, it'll take all the strength God can give you to do it. You're also apt to meet some sincere Christian guys serving time, and you can be of real help to each other."

It was good advice from a young man who really knew from experience, and Ken genuinely appreciated it.

While planning for his future, Ken even found some time to relax. One afternoon when he was out driving in the city, he picked up two young men hitchhiking and offered to take them to their destination several miles out of his way. Ken thought there just might be a chance to share a witness for Christ, something he had scoffed at in earlier times when he had been given rides before meeting the Lord.

The pair were most grateful for the ride until one of them noted Ken's name on a paper on the car seat. The youth suddenly paled and asked haltingly, "Are you Ken Pestana, *the* Ken Pestana?"

"Why, yes," Ken answered casually.

"Hey, do me a favor, will you?" the rider asked nervoulsy. "Just pull over to the corner up ahead and let us out. I think, well, I guess we'd rather walk, okay?"

Ken let the youths out and drove off, not really surprised but still disappointed at the experience. "I was only trying to be a good Samaritan," Ken sadly volunteered, "But then I guess he wasn't in the headlines and out on bail when he stopped to help."

As sentencing day approached, the judge received a report on the case and the personal history of the defendants carefully prepared by a probation officer.

On Al there was little to report beyond the details of the crime, the history of alcoholism in his family, and the fact that some of the violence in this young man may have been triggered by the death of his girl friend in an automobile accident about a month before the robbery. Al refused to talk to the court officer, thus passing up the opportunity to get his feelings in writing before the judge.

The report on Ken was more complex. The extent of his involvement and knowledge of the robbery and killing was open to some question, the changes in his life since the time of the crime had to be considered, and there were a number of possible sentencing alternatives that could be recommended on a second degree murder conviction.

The young probation officer who prepared the report thoroughly reviewed all the records of the investigation, added an interview with

Ken, and quickly zeroed in on what the officer believed was the central issue in deciding his recommendation—the degree of Ken's participation in the tragedy. Ken was carefully quizzed about this, and the officer concluded that Ken was a knowing and willing partner in the robbery that became a murder, a belief the officer firmly maintained when Ken's attorneys suggested there was nothing in the evidence to justify such a conclusion.

"There is also nothing in the reports that contradicts my view," the probation officer countered. Thus he would tell the court that Ken as well as Al "was basically responsible for the offenses, including the death of the victim" and should be sent to prison.

There was an additional informative document before the court, the psychological evaluation prepared by Lois Mark. Her study noted "Ken's past negative behavior did bring him attention but usually in a negative vein, thus reinforcing his poor self-image."

In contrast to Ken's past conduct and poor view of himself, the report then noted, "An outstanding factor to his advantage at this crucial point in his life has been his conversion to Christianity and the structure and goal direction it has given him."

The counselor concluded by stressing the probable negative effects of an adult penal incarceration for Ken and urged the judge to place him in a youth educational and rehabilitation facility.

There were also fine letters of recommendation for Kenny presented to the judge from people who knew and appreciated the young man's stand for the Lord and the obvious change in his life.

But there were also a number of impressive, well-written letters telling the judge of the fine character and reputation of the murdered victim in this case. "His life was one of happiness, joy and zest in living," wrote his former high school counselor. A neighbor described him as a "credit to himself, his family, school and community." A girl friend told the judge, "When he departed from this earth, he left enough good memories for his friends to remember for years to come." Yet another young lady referred to the interest of the youth in children, "He was always fond of them, took time to be with them, and took time to be interested." A baseball coach described the young man who had died as "one of the finest individuals I have met in my years of teaching and coaching."

Finding it difficult to put her feelings into words, the mother of the murdered youth wrote the district attorney, "I do hope with all my heart that the young men responsible for this tragedy realize what happens to a family because of an inhuman act such as they committed."

"The taking of any human life is a tragedy," the district attorney told me, "but it seems even more so when the victim is such a decent, fine, talented young man with his whole life ahead of him." There was no doubt as to why the prosecutor would ask the judge to send both Ken and Al to prison.

The night before sentencing, Ken and I reviewed the case at length. "What do you think will happen tomorrow?" Ken suddenly asked. It was not an easy question for me to answer.

"I don't know, Ken. It's hard to know what a judge is thinking. But with all the facts about the case and background on you personally before him, and the knowledge that you were not armed, nor in the store that evening, nor even saw the victim, I believe the judge can draw a clear line of distinction between you and Al. Despite his being urged to do so, I cannot conceive of the judge sending you to prison.

"But remember, that's only my opinion. The outcome is not in our hands. We can't control the turn of events. All we can do is ask God for power in your life to go through whatever may be ahead. He has not promised us easy ways out of our problems, but He has promised His strength when we need it to go through adversity."

Ken agreed and we prayed together.

The next morning driving to court, Ken heard a radio news report telling of another young felon who had been sentenced from local court to state prison. He was now dead of thirteen stab wounds less than two weeks after his arrival. This man had been confined for burglary, auto theft and forgery, and he was the eighth fatality in sixty stabbing incidents at the particular prison in ten months. Ken quickly dialed to another station.

As court opened, Al's counsel made a short statement on behalf of his client. After Mr. Pestarino had simply but forcefully urged the court to commit Ken to a youth facility, Ken braced himself for what he was sure would be a strong, harsh argument from the district attorney.

Mr. Davies was surprisingly soft-spoken and brief, but his position was very firm. He mentioned the victim would like to be alive to trade places even in a prison cell with the accused. Then he carefully linked Al and Ken together in the criminal acts of that fateful night. "Both men are responsible for the death here, both committed the offense. Mr. Pestana got a second degree murder conviction and with that achieved justice with a measure of mercy. But now, your honor, if the younger man must go to prison, then so should Mr. Pestana."

He did not mention that the third youth involved, one year older than Al, had already been sent to the Youth Authority by juvenile court. The arguments were over.

The courtroom was tense as the judge prepared to announce his ruling. It was obvious from both his serious expression and careful speech that the judge considered imposition of sentence in this case a most distasteful responsibility.

First he ordered Al to state prison for the term prescribed by law for first degree murder—life imprisonment. Al expected that and took the verdict calmly. He whispered to his public defender that he wanted to stay in the courtroom for the disposition of Ken's case. The judge appeared a little surprised but Al stayed.

The judge looked directly at Ken and his attorneys seated at the defense counsel table. "If this crime were not so serious, I would be most inclined to grant your recommendation for state Youth Authority.

"But I cannot do that in this case. Mr. Pestana, too, will be sentenced to the department of corrections for the term prescribed by law for second degree murder: Prison. Five years to life."

The spectators in the courtroom could hardly believe what they were hearing. For Ken the words of judgment fell like blows from a sledge hammer. His mouth dried, his muscles tensed, and he felt sick inside. The judge was not through.

"I will direct that if the state prison diagnostic center feels that a placement other than prison is more suitable, they may so inform the court, and I will consider such a recommendation. That is all."

The judge gathered his notes, stood up, and quickly exited.

Ken talked briefly with his attorney before being escorted from the courtroom by two deputy sheriffs.

Ken was gone before the full impact of the unexpected sentence had been felt by his family and friends in the courtroom. Slowly and quietly the onlookers got up, talked in hushed tones to each other, as if at a funeral, and then cleared the courtroom. The judge was due to return in a few minutes to continue the trial of two other teen-agers charged in another murder case.

"Did you ever consider that Ken may have been penalized because he comes from a wealthy family who could afford the best counsel?" an observer asked me outside the courtroom.

"If his people had been poor, he might have been handled differently, but it could well be the court leaned over backwards to show that the prominent or successful will not get off lightly."

I didn't know if that was a factor or not in the decision. I just know I was tremendously disappointed.

A few hours later Ken was returned to murder max row in the county jail, now waiting transfer to prison. As he was brought out to talk with me, once again he wore the hideous orange jump suit, the handcuffs and shackles that mark a prisoner in this jail as a dangerous felon. For six months of visiting Ken in jail I had seen him in chains, but the four months he was out on bail where we had communicated casually in freedom made me tend to forget Ken would once again be returned to shackles and a cell. To see my friend so confined was a shocking, unwelcome reminder of the reality of his plight.

Earlier that day I had talked with Ken's partner, Frank, who was also in custody on several charges. He had been sitting in his cell reading the first part of this book, and he had strong feelings about it.

"I've been Kenny's tightest partner in crime and otherwise for several years. We're just like brothers, and I can tell you he is a changed man.

"After he was released on bond and was on the outs, he told me about the Lord and said he was going God's way. I remember telling him at the time, 'You're crazy, man; you're going to prison!' His response was, 'Then that's all the more reason to be in tight with the Lord.' I just shook my head and we went our separate ways.

"But even then I was so very happy for Ken because he had found something that changed his life for the better. And have no doubt about it, he's sincere."

"And what about you, Frank" I asked the seventeen-year-old youth, sharp, intelligent, but in much trouble and facing trial as an adult. He hesitated before answering, as if to weigh every word.

"I've done everything you and Kenny put in the book, and a lot more. To tell you the truth, I'm still a long ways from getting things put together in my own life. I wish I could hang up my guns, get things right, and figure out where I'm headed. Right now I just don't know."

"You can get it together, Frank, and Ken told you how—with the Lord," I responded. "I know," he replied softly as we shook hands and ended our visit.

I told Kenny of my visit with Frank, and concern for his buddy came as a welcome, if only temporary, relief from his own heavy concerns.

It was apparent that he was still in a state of emotional shock from the events of the morning, groping for an explanation to ease his troubled mind.

It would have been so much better if the probation officer who made the prison recommendation, the district attorney who argued for

The moment Ken dreaded is here. The trial is over and Ken is ordered to prison.

it, or even the judge who handed down the sentence had sat across the jail counsel table from Ken that night to explain a judgment they undoubtedly felt was right. Instead, the responsibility fell to me, and it was certainly beyond my ability to sound convincing in justifying the whys of what I considered an unduly harsh, unwarranted sentence.

It was a little more difficult to explain in view of my respect for the professional conduct of the three men responsible for the decision, especially the judge. Perhaps more important, Ken especially admired the judge, and this only made his order in the case so much harder for the young defendant to accept or even understand. That the judge may yet modify his sentence after the prison diagnostic review doesn't relieve Ken's pressures at the moment.

As we quietly talked, Ken spent long periods silently looking down at his shackled wrists. He was struggling desperately to find a way to grasp fully something neither of us believed was right.

After one such pause, he looked up and carefully commented, "I guess God hasn't gone out of business. He's still with me. It's going to be rough, but I want to make it. And if the Lord is with me, I can come out all right." He smiled slightly for the first time that evening.

He was feeling deeply every word he said.

"Yes, Ken," I replied slowly, "as long as you have the Lord, you can make it."

And so can each of us who know HIM.

EPILOGUE

A Personal Message from Ken Pestana

It's all here. You got a good look at me as I was and what happened to make things different. Just think what a hopeless, sick story this would have been if the Lord hadn't stepped in.

When I became a Christian, God took away 95 percent of my language and nearly all my old friends, though I don't think that was a big loss. You see, in place of my old partners, He gave me a new warm relationship with my family and with so many of His people. I really gained on the trade.

I lost a lot of things when I met the Lord: a gangster brim, an ear ring, a swastika, cycle-gang colors, a cocky style, a lousy attitude, a filthy mouth and a bad temper. That's just for openers.

The important thing is that the Lord added far more to my life than anything He took away. I got rid of a mess of sins and picked up on some real peace inside. He added a heavy dose of love, forgiveness, and a sense of real worth— not the phony stuff. And it sure beats carrying around a piece to prove you're a big man.

Another strange thing: I don't rip off people anymore. It was wierd for me to go to work and earn the money to buy something that I could hiest in a few seconds. My old partners were amazed at my sudden attack of honesty and were afraid it just might be permanent. Well it is, and I'm just as amazed as they are. Worse, they thought it might be contagious, so most of them cut out. Getting into the Lord does wild things to a guy. Now I actually care how my actions will affect other people. That's gotta be an improvement.

Don't think I'm some super saint. I'm not. I didn't pick up a shining halo because I dropped the black brim. I don't always think the sharpest, and I still do some dumb things. And let me tell you, the pressure from the haps in court was a heavy thing on my mind. But the Lord helped me to get through it so much better than I could have before. He's taught me a lot of things about His way of life in order to make me a better guy.

Before I went to prison, I saw a lot of people my age around. Some were into the Lord and going great; others at least will be good citizens. But I saw too many who are starting out the way I did: cutting school, using dope, doing rip-offs, into juvie, and then up the line to big trouble. And I care about them.

Today I'm where many people think I ought to be—locked up. There is no point in arguing about it. I'm here. But I'll be out again, and I pray that God will help me to make it on the streets. I'd like to get into my dad's business and use the coin I make to help young people find the Lord. I really like the Campus Life work among the high schools and the work to reach kids who are starting out in trouble. Someday I plan to get in and help.

That's only the beginning. There's a song that says, "If you believe in forever, then this life is just a one-night stand." So I have problems here. Forever is a long time, and I'm glad I'm going to spend it with the Lord. Then the problems will be over.

As you read this book you likely decided what you think about me: young punk, cheap hoodlum who ought to be locked up while they throw the key away, tough guy trying to survive, or bad kid who changed. Take your choice. All those things have been true. However it comes out in the end, I'll have to face up to it with God.

Now what about you? You've got your own problems, right?

I'm no hot-shot expert on the Bible, but I know the Lord can meet the needs of anyone who honestly comes to Him. I believe that so much that I've said I'd rather be in prison with the Lord than out on the streets the way I was before, without Him. And that's straight goods.

I had to blow it real bad before God got to me. I hope you pass up that trip and open your life to Him. It'll be the best move you ever made.

I know that's true because my life is so much like a guy in the Bible named Paul who wrote from prison, "God had mercy on me so that Christ Jesus could use me as an example to show everyone how patient He is with even the worst sinners, so that others will realize that they, too, can have everlasting life" (1 Timothy 2:16).

Any takers?

Ken Pestana

Ken Pestana

A 16 mm color motion picture dramatizing the Ken Pestana story and featuring Ken as himself is now available. Ask for *Devil at the Wheel* at your religious film library. The film was produced for Family Films, 5823 Santa Monica Boulevard, Hollywood, California 90038, through the facilities of Johnson-Nyquist Productions.